The Indwelling Spirit

Andrew Murray

D1714963

BOOKS BY ANDREW MURRAY
FROM BETHANY HOUSE PUBLISHERS
With Updated Language

Abiding in Christ
Absolute Surrender
The Andrew Murray Daily Reader
The Believer's Call to Commitment
The Believer's Daily Renewal
Believing Prayer
The Blood of Christ
The Fullness of the Spirit
Humility
The Indwelling Spirit
A Life of Obedience
Living a Prayerful Life
The Ministry of Intercessory Prayer
The Path to Holiness
Teach Me to Pray

The Indwelling Spirit

Andrew Murray

BETHANYHOUSE
Minneapolis, Minnesota

The Indwelling Spirit
by Andrew Murray

Copyright © 1979, 2006
Bethany House Publishers

Previously published under the title *The Spirit of Christ*
The 2006 version has been edited and condensed.

Cover design by Eric Walljasper

Italics in quoted Scripture represents emphasis by the author.

All Scripture quotations are from the New King James Version of the Bible.
Copyright © 1979, 1980, 1982 by Thomas Nelson, Inc. Used by permission. All
rights reserved.

Published by Bethany House Publishers
11400 Hampshire Avenue South
Bloomington, Minnesota 55438

Bethany House Publishers is a division of
Baker Publishing Group, Grand Rapids, Michigan.

Printed in the United States of America

ISBN-13: 978-0-7642-0227-8
ISBN-10: 0-7642-0227-8

Library of Congress Cataloging-in-Publication Data

Murray, Andrew, 1828-1917.
    The indwelling Spirit : the work of the Holy Spirit in the life of the believer
/ by Andrew Murray. — Edited and condensed.
        p.   cm.
    Summary: "A study on the person and work of the Holy Spirit, third
person of the Trinity, in the life of the Christian"—Provided by publisher.
    Rev. ed. of: The Spirit of Christ.
    ISBN 0-7642-0227-8 (pbk.)
1. Holy Spirit—Sermons. 2. Sermons, English. 3. Reformed Church—
Sermons. I. Murray, Andrew, 1828-1917. Spirit of Christ. II. Title.
    BT122 .M87   2006
    231'.3—dc22

                                                                            2006013577

ANDREW MURRAY was born in South Africa in 1828. After receiving his education in Scotland and Holland, he returned to South Africa and spent many years as both pastor and missionary. He was a staunch advocate of biblical Christianity, and is best known for his many devotional books.

Preface

Throughout time there have been believers who have met God, known Him, and through faith have had the assurance that they were well-pleasing to God. When the Son of God came to earth, revealing the Father, His purpose was that fellowship with God and the assurance of His favor might become the abiding joy of every child of God. When He was exalted to the throne of glory after His resurrection, it was so that He might send the Holy Spirit to abide in us, that we might know true fellowship with God. It was to be one of the marks of the new covenant that each member of it should walk in personal communion with God.

> No more shall every man teach his neighbor, and every man his brother, saying, "Know the Lord," for they all shall know Me, from the least of them to the greatest of them, says the Lord. For I will forgive their iniquity, and their sin I will remember no more. (Jeremiah 31:34)

Personal fellowship and knowledge of God through the Holy Spirit was to be the result of pardon from sin. The Spirit of God's own Son was sent into our hearts to do a work as divine as that of redemption. The Spirit replaces our life with the life of Christ, in power, making the Son of God consciously present with us. This was the distinctive blessing of the New Testament. The fellowship of God, the three-in-one, was to be *within us,* the Spirit revealing the Son, and through Him, the Father.

Few believers realize the walk with God that their Father has prepared for them. And fewer are willing to discuss what the cause of the failure might be. We must acknowledge that the Holy Spirit, through whose divine omnipotence this inner revelation comes, is not fully realized in the church—the body of Christ—as He should be. In our preaching and in our practice He does not hold the place of prominence He has in God's plan. While our belief in the Holy Spirit may be orthodox and scriptural, His presence and power in the life of believers, in the ministry of the Word, in the witness of the church to the world, is not what the Word promises or God's plan requires.

There are many who are conscious of this lack and earnestly ask to know God's mind concerning it and the way of deliverance from it. Some feel that their own life is not what it should be. Many can look back to a special season of spiritual revival when their whole life was on a higher plain. The experience of the joy and strength of the Savior's presence was for a time very real. But it did not last. For many there has been a gradual decline, accompanied by vain efforts and subsequent failure. Some long to know where the problem lies. There is little doubt as to the answer: They do not know or honor the indwelling Spirit as the strength of their life, the power of their faith to keep them looking to Jesus and trusting in Him. They do not know what it is to day by day wait in quiet confidence for the Holy Spirit to deliver them from the power of the flesh and to maintain the wonderful presence of the Father and the Son.

There are multitudes of God's dear children who still experience a never-ending stumbling and rising in their spiritual lives. In spite of revivals, seminars, and conferences, the teaching they receive is not particularly helpful in the matter of entire consecration. Their everyday surroundings are not favorable to the growth of the spiritual life. There may be times of longing to live according to the full will of God, but the prospect of actually walking well-pleasing to Him has hardly dawned on them. They are strangers to the best part of their birthright as God's children, to the most precious gift of the Father's love in Christ—the gift of the Holy Spirit, who desires to dwell in them and lead them.

I would count it an unspeakable privilege if God would use me to address to these, His beloved children, the question found in His Word: "Do you not know that you are the temple of God and that the Spirit of God dwells in you?" (1 Corinthians 3:16) and then to tell them what that glorious work is that the Spirit is able to do in and through them. I would like to show them what it is that has no doubt hindered the Spirit from doing His blessed work. I would explain how simple the path is by which each upright soul can enter into the joy of the full revelation of the presence of the indwelling Jesus. I have humbly asked God that He would give through my simple words the quickening of His Holy Spirit so that through them the truth, love, and power of God might enter into the hearts of many of His children. I long that these words may bring in reality and experience the wondrous gift of love they describe—the life and joy of the Holy Spirit as He reveals to them the Lord Jesus, whom until now they may have known only from afar.

I must confess to still another hope. I have a strong

fear—and I say it in all humility—that in the theology of our churches, the teaching and leading of the Spirit of truth, the anointing that alone teaches all things, is not recognized in a practical sense. If the leaders of our churches—the teachers, pastors, Bible scholars, writers, and layworkers—were all fully conscious of the fact that in everything that concerns the Word of God and the church of Christ the Holy Spirit should have the supreme place of honor as He did in the Acts of the Apostles, surely the signs and marks of His presence would be clearer and His mighty works more manifest. I trust I have not been presumptuous in hoping that what has been written here may help to remind even our spiritual leaders of that which is so easily overlooked—the indispensable requirement for what is to bear fruit for eternity: to be full of the power of the eternal Spirit.

I am well aware of what may be expected by men of intellect and culture, by true theologians, that these writings should bear the marks of scholarship, force of thought, and power of expression. To these I cannot dare to lay claim. Yet I venture to ask any of these honored brethren who may read these lines to regard the book at least as the echo of a cry for light rising from many hearts and as a display of questions, the solution for which many are longing. There is a prevalent feeling that Christ's promise of what the church should be and its actual present state do not correspond.

Of all theological questions, there is none that leads us more deeply into the glory of God or that is of more intense, vital, and practical importance for daily life than that which deals with the full revelation of God and the work of redemption—or in what way and to what extent God's Holy Spirit can dwell in, fill, and make into a holy and beautiful temple of God, the heart of His child, making Christ reign there as the ever-present and almighty Savior. It is a question of which the solution, if it were sought and found in the presence and teaching of the Spirit himself, would transform all our theology into that knowledge of God which is eternal life.

We have no lack of theology in every possible form. But it seems that with all our writing and preaching and work, there is still something lacking. Is it not the power from on high? Could it be that with all our love for Christ and labor for His cause we have not made the chief object of our desire that which was the chief object of His heart when He ascended to the throne? It was to clothe His disciples with the power of the Holy Spirit—that knowing again the presence of their Lord, they might become powerful witnesses of Him. May God raise up from among our theologians many who will dedicate their lives to see that God's Holy Spirit is recognized in the lives of believers, in the ministry of the Word by tongue and pen, and in all the work done in His church.

I have noticed with deep interest a new emphasis on unity in prayer—that Christian life and teaching may be increasingly subject to the Holy Spirit. I believe that one of the first blessings of this united prayer will be to direct attention to the reasons why prayer is not more visibly answered as well as preparation for receiving answers to prayer. In my reading on this subject as well as my observation of the lives of believers and my own personal experience, I have been deeply impressed with one thought: Our prayer for the work of the Holy Spirit through us can only be answered as His indwelling in every believer is acknowledged and lived out. We have the Holy Spirit within us; only he who is faithful in the small things will receive the greater. As we first yield ourselves to be led by the Spirit, to confess His presence in us, and as every believer realizes and accepts His guidance in his daily life, God will entrust to us larger measures of His work. If we give ourselves entirely to His ruling within us, He will give more of himself to us and work through us.

My one desire is that the Lord will use what I have written to make clear and impress on every reader this truth: It is as our *indwelling* life that the Holy Spirit must be known. In a living, adoring faith, the Spirit's indwelling must be accepted and treasured until it becomes part of the consciousness of the new person in Christ: The Holy Spirit possesses me. In this faith, the whole life, even in the smallest things, must be surrendered to His leading, while all that is of the flesh or self must die. If in this faith we wait on God for His divine leading and working, placing ourselves entirely at His disposal, our prayer cannot remain unanswered. There will be manifestations of the Spirit's power in the church and the world such as we could not dare to hope. The Holy Spirit only requires vessels that are entirely set apart to Him. He delights to manifest in us the glory of Christ our Lord.

I commit each beloved fellow believer to the teaching of the Holy Spirit. May we all, as we study His work, be partakers of the anointing that teaches us all things.

—Andrew Murray

Contents

Chapter 1

A New Spirit, and God's Spirit

I will give you a new heart and put a new spirit within you; I will take the heart of stone out of your flesh and give you a heart of flesh. I will put My Spirit within you and cause you to walk in My statutes, and you will keep My judgments and do them.

Ezekiel 36:26–27

God has revealed himself in two great dispensations. In the old we have the time of promise and preparation, in the new, fulfillment and possession. In harmony with the difference between the two dispensations, there is a twofold working of God's Spirit. In the Old Testament we have the Spirit of God coming upon people and working in them in special times and ways: working from above, without, and within. In the New Testament we have the Holy Spirit entering them and dwelling within them: working from within, without, and upward. In the former we have the Spirit of God as the Almighty and Holy One; in the latter we have the Spirit of the Father of Jesus Christ.

The difference between the twofold working of the Holy Spirit is not to be regarded as though with the closing of the Old Testament the former ceased and in the New there was no more work of preparation. Not at all. Just as there were in the Old Testament blessed anticipations of the indwelling of God's Spirit, so now in the New Testament the twofold working still continues. Because of a lack of knowledge, faith, or faithfulness, a believer today may receive little more than the Old Testament measure of the Spirit's working. The indwelling Spirit has indeed been given to every child of God, and yet he may experience little more than the first half of the promise. A new spirit is given to us in regeneration, but we may know almost nothing of God's Spirit as a living person dwelling within us. The Spirit's work in convincing us of sin and of righteousness, in His leading to repentance and faith and the new life, is the preparatory work. The distinctive glory of the dispensation of the Spirit is His divine personal indwelling in the heart of the believer, where He is able to fully reveal to him the Father and the Son. It is only as Christians understand this that they will be able to claim the full blessing prepared for them in Christ Jesus.

In the words of Ezekiel we find very strikingly set forth in one promise the twofold blessing God bestows through His Spirit. The first is: "I will . . . put *a new spirit* within you"—that is, our own spirit is to be renewed and quickened by God's Spirit. When this has been done, there is the second blessing: "I will put *My Spirit* within you," to dwell in that new spirit. God must dwell in a habitation. He had to create Adam's body before He could breathe the spirit of life into him. In Israel, the tabernacle and the temple had to be completed before God could take possession of them. Likewise, a new heart is given and a new spirit put within us as the indispensable condition of God's own Spirit dwelling within us. We find the same contrast in David's prayer: First, "Create in me a clean heart, O God, and renew a steadfast spirit within me"; then, "Do not take Your Holy Spirit from me" (Psalm 51:10–11). Look what is indicated in the words "That which is born of the Spirit is spirit" (John 3:6): There is the divine Spirit giving birth to the new spirit. The two are also distinguished: "The Spirit Himself bears witness with our spirit that we are children of God" (Romans 8:16). Our spirit is the renewed, regenerate spirit. God's Spirit dwells in our spirit, yet distinguished from it, witnesses in, with, and through it.

The importance of recognizing this distinction can easily be perceived. We will then be able to understand the true connection between regeneration and the indwelling of the Spirit. The former is the work of the Holy Spirit by which He convinces us of sin, leads us to repentance and faith in Christ, and imparts to us a new nature. The believer becomes a child of God, a temple fit for the Spirit to dwell in. Where faith claims it, the second half of the promise is fulfilled as surely as the first. However, as long as the believer looks only at regeneration and the renewal wrought in his spirit, he will not come to the life of joy and strength that is intended. But when he accepts God's promise that there is something more than the new nature, that there is the Spirit of the Father and the Son to dwell within him, there opens up a wonderful prospect of holiness and blessedness. His desire will be to know this Holy Spirit, how He works, and what He asks of us, and to know how he may experience His indwelling and the revelation of the Son of God, which is His work to bestow.

Of course, the question is often asked, "How are these two parts of the divine promise fulfilled—simultaneously or successively?" The answer is very simple: From God's side the twofold gift is simultaneous. The Spirit is not divided: In giving the Spirit, God gives himself and all He is. It was so on the day of Pentecost: The three thousand received a new spirit with repentance and faith, and on the same day they were baptized they received the indwelling Spirit as God's seal to their faith. Through the word of the disciples, the Spirit did a mighty work among the multitudes, changing dispositions, hearts, and spirits. When in the power of this new spirit working in them they had believed and confessed, they received the baptism of the Holy Spirit as well.

Today when the Spirit of God moves mightily and the church is living in the power of the Spirit, the converts that are born receive from the first beginnings of their Christian life the distinct, conscious sealing and indwelling of the Spirit. But we have indications in Scripture that there may be circumstances, dependent either on the anointing of the preacher or the faith of the hearers, in which the two halves of the promise are not so closely linked. It was so with the believers in Samaria converted under Philip's preaching as well as with the converts Paul met at Ephesus. In these cases the experience of the apostles themselves was repeated. They were regarded as regenerate men before our Lord's death, but it was at Pentecost that the further promise was fulfilled: "And they were all filled with the Holy Spirit" (Acts 2:4). What was seen in them—the grace of the Spirit divided into two separate manifestations—may still occur today.

When neither in the preaching of the Word nor in the testimony of believers is the truth of an indwelling Spirit distinctly proclaimed, we must not wonder why His Spirit is known and experienced only as the Spirit of regeneration. His indwelling presence will remain a mystery. Even when the Spirit of Christ in all His fullness is bestowed once for all as an indwelling Spirit, He is received and possessed only as far as the faith of the believer reaches.

The Spirit first works from without on and in believers in word and deed before He dwells in them and becomes their inner personal possession. We must distinguish between the in-working and the indwelling of the Spirit.

It is generally acknowledged in the church that the Holy Spirit does not receive the recognition that belongs to Him as being equal with the Father and the Son. He is, after all, the divine person through whom alone the Father and the Son can be truly possessed and known. At the time of the Reformation, the gospel of Christ had to be vindicated from the terrible misapprehension that made man's righteousness the ground of his acceptance. The freedom of divine grace had to be maintained. To the ages that followed was committed the trust of building on that foundation and promoting what the riches of grace would do for the believer. The church has rested contentedly in what it has received, and the teaching of what the Holy Spirit will do for each believer through guiding, sanctifying, and strengthening has not taken the place it ought to have in our teaching and in our living. In fact, if we review the history of the church, we will notice how many important truths, clearly revealed in Scripture, have been allowed to lie dormant, unknown and unappreciated except by a few isolated Christians.

Let us pray that God in His power may grant a mighty working of the Spirit in His church, that each child of God may prove that the double promise is fulfilled: "I will ... put a new spirit within you; I will put My Spirit within you." Pray that we may so apprehend the wonderful blessing of the indwelling Spirit that our whole being may be opened up to the full revelation of the Father's love and the grace of Jesus Christ.

This twice-repeated word of our text—"within you; within you"—is one of the key words of the new covenant. The word translated *within* is not a preposition, but the same as is rendered here and elsewhere "inward part" and "inner thought" (Psalm 5:9; 49:11). "I will put My fear *in their hearts* so that they will not depart from Me" (Jeremiah 32:40). God created man's heart for His dwelling. Sin entered and defiled it. God's Spirit strove to regain possession. In the incarnation and atonement of Christ the redemption was accomplished and the kingdom of God established. Jesus could say, "The kingdom of God is *within you*" (Luke 17:21). It is *within* that we must look for the fulfillment of the new covenant, the covenant not of ordinances but of life. In the power of an endless life the law and the fear of God are to be stamped upon our hearts; the Spirit of Christ himself is to be within us as the power of our life. Not only on Calvary, or in the resurrection, or on the throne is the glory of Christ the conqueror to be seen— but *in our heart*. Within us is to be the true display of the reality and the glory of His redemption. Within us, in our inmost being, is the hidden sanctuary where the ark of the covenant is sprinkled with the blood. It contains the law written in an ever-living script by the indwelling Spirit, and where, through the Spirit, the Father and the Son now come to dwell.

O my God! I do thank you for this double blessing. I thank you for that wonderful holy temple you have built up in me for yourself—a new spirit given within me. And I thank you for that still more wonderful holy presence, your own Spirit, to dwell within me and there reveal the Father and the Son to me.

I do pray that you will open my eyes to the mystery of your love. Let the words within you *bring me to my knees in trembling fear before your condescension and may my one desire be to have my spirit indeed be the worthy dwelling of your Spirit. Let them lift me up in holy trust and expectation to look for and claim all that your promise means.*

O Father, I thank you that your Spirit dwells within me. May my daily walk be in the deep reverence of His holy presence with me and the glad experience of all He works in and through me. Amen.

Summary

1. Here we have the reason why many fail in their effort to abide in Christ, to walk like Christ, to live holy in Christ. They do not fully know the wonderful all-sufficient provision God has made to enable them to do so. They do not have the clear assurance that the Holy Spirit will work in them and through them all that is needed.

2. The distinction between a new spirit and His Spirit

within me is of deepest importance. In the new spirit given to me, I have a work of God in me; in God's Spirit dwelling in me, I have God himself, a living person. What a difference between having a home built by a rich friend and given me and having the rich friend come to live with me and fulfill my every need and want!

3. The Spirit is given both as a builder and as an inhabitant of our temple. We cannot live until He builds, and He builds that He may dwell with us.

4. There must be harmony between a home and its occupant. The more I know this holy Guest, the more I will give my inmost being to Him to order, to lead, and to adorn as pleases Him.

5. The Holy Spirit is the true expression of the Father and the Son. My spirit is the true expression of myself. The Holy Spirit renews that inmost self, then dwells in it and fills it. He becomes to me what He was to Jesus—the very life of my personality.

Chapter 2

The Baptism
of the Spirit

And John bore witness, saying, "I saw the Spirit
descending from heaven like a dove, and He remained
upon Him. I did not know Him, but He who sent me to
baptize with water said to me, 'Upon whom you see the
Spirit descending, and remaining on Him, this is He
who baptizes with the Holy Spirit.'"

John 1:32–33

There were two things that John the Baptist preached concerning the person of Christ: First, He was the Lamb of God who takes away the sin of the world, and second, He would baptize His disciples with the Holy Spirit and with fire. The blood of the Lamb and the baptism of the Spirit were the two central truths of his creed and his preaching. They are, indeed, inseparable: The church cannot do her work in power, nor can her exalted Lord be glorified in her unless the blood as the foundation-stone and the Spirit as the cornerstone are fully preached.

This has not always been done, even among those who wholeheartedly accept Scripture as their guide. The preaching of the Lamb of God, His suffering and atonement, pardon and peace through Him, is more easily grasped and more readily influences our feelings than the spiritual truth of the baptism, indwelling, and guidance of the Holy Spirit. The pouring out of Christ's blood took place on earth; it was something visible and outward, and by virtue of the types, not altogether unintelligible. The pouring out of the Spirit took place in heaven, a divine and hidden mystery. The shedding of the blood was for the ungodly and rebellious; the gift of the Spirit, for the loving and obedient disciple. It is no wonder that the church, often lacking in love and obedience, finds it harder to receive the truth of the baptism of the Spirit than that of redemption and forgiveness.

And yet God would not have it so. The Old Testament promise speaks of God's Spirit within us. The forerunner (John the Baptist) took up the strain and did not preach the atoning Lamb without telling us to what extent we were to be redeemed and how God's high purpose was to be fulfilled in us. Sin brought not only guilt and condemnation but defilement and death. It incurred not only loss of God's favor but made us unfit for divine fellowship. Without fellowship, the Love that created man could not be content. God wanted us for himself—our heart and affection, our inmost personality, our true self—a home for His love, a temple for His worship. The preaching of John included both the beginning and the end of redemption: The blood of the Lamb was to cleanse God's temple and restore His throne within the heart. Nothing less than the baptism and indwelling of the Spirit can satisfy the heart of God or man.

Jesus would give only what He received. Because the Spirit rested on Him when He was baptized, He could baptize with the Spirit. The Spirit descending and abiding on Him meant He had been born of the Holy Spirit; in the power of the Spirit He had grown up; He had entered manhood free from sin, and now had come to John to fulfill all the law of righteousness by submitting to the baptism of repentance, even though He had not sinned. As a reward of His obedience, He had the Father's seal of approval. He received a new communication of the power of the heavenly life. Beyond what He had already experienced, the Father's indwelling presence and power took possession of Him and equipped Him for His work. The leading and the power of the Spirit became His more consciously than before (Luke 4:1, 14, 22); He was now anointed with the Holy Spirit and with power.

Though baptized himself, He could not yet baptize others. First, in the power of His baptism, He had to face temptation and overcome it. He had to learn obedience and suffer, and through the eternal Spirit offer himself a sacrifice unto God and His will—only then would He receive the Holy Spirit as the reward of obedience (Acts 2:33) with the power to baptize all who belong to Him.

Jesus' life teaches us what the baptism of the Spirit is. It is more than the grace by which we turn to God, are saved, and seek to live as God's children. When Jesus reminded His disciples of John's prophecy (Acts 1:4–5), they were already partakers of grace. Their baptism with the Spirit meant something more. It was to be the conscious presence of the glorified Lord come back from heaven to dwell in their hearts. And it was their participation in the power of His new life. It was a baptism of joy and power. All that they were to receive of wisdom, courage, and holiness had its root in this: What the Spirit was to Jesus when He was baptized, the living bond with the Father's power and presence, He was to be to the disciples. Through the Spirit, the Son would manifest himself, and Father and Son would make their home with them.

"Upon whom you see the Spirit descending, and remaining on him, this is He who baptizes with the Holy Spirit" (John 1:33). This word is to us as well as to John. To know what the baptism of the Spirit means and how we are to receive it, we must look at the One upon whom the Spirit descended and rested. We must see Jesus baptized with the Holy Spirit. He needed it, was prepared for it, yielded himself to it. It was through the power of the Holy Spirit that He gave His life and then was raised from the dead. What Jesus has to give us, He first received and personally appropriated; what He received and won for himself was all for us. Let Him make it yours.

In regard to this baptism of the Spirit, there are questions that arise. Everyone will not have the same answer. Was the outpouring of the Spirit at Pentecost the complete fulfillment of the promise? Was that the only baptism of the Spirit, given once for all to the newborn church? Or is the coming of the Holy Spirit on the disciples (Acts 4); on the Samaritans (Acts 8); on the heathen in the house of Cornelius (Acts 10); and on the twelve disciples at Ephesus (Acts 19) also to be regarded as separate fulfillments of the words: "He will baptize with the Holy Spirit"? Is the sealing of the Spirit, given to each believer in regeneration, to be counted as a baptism of the Spirit? Or is it, as some say, a distinct, individual blessing to be received at a later date? Is it a blessing given only once or can it be repeated and renewed? In the course of our study, God's Word will shed light on these questions. But at the outset we should not allow ourselves to be overly preoccupied with them. Rather, we should fix our hearts on the great spiritual lessons that God would have us learn from the preaching of the baptism of the Holy Spirit. There are two in particular.

The first is that the baptism of the Holy Spirit is the crown and glory of Jesus' work, and we must acknowledge this if we are to live the true Christian life. Jesus needed it. Christ's obedient disciples needed it. It is more than the working of the Spirit in regeneration. It is the personal Spirit of Christ present within us, abiding in the heart in the power of His glorified nature. It is the Spirit of the life of Christ Jesus making us free from the law of sin and death and bringing us, by personal experience, into the freedom from sin for which Christ redeemed us. To many it is perceived as a blessing given on our behalf, though not actually owned by the believer. But it is this power that fills us with boldness in the presence of temptation and gives us victory over the world and the enemy. It is the fulfillment of what God meant when He said, "I will dwell in them and walk among them" (2 Corinthians 6:16).

The second lesson is that it is Jesus who baptizes us. Whether we look upon this baptism as something we already have and of which we only need a firmer grasp, or something we still must receive, all will agree: It is only in relationship with Jesus, in faithful fellowship and obedience to Him, that a Spirit-filled life can be maintained. "He who believes in Me," Jesus said, "out of his heart will flow rivers of living water" (John 7:38). We need a living faith in the indwelling Jesus. Faith is the instinct of the new nature that recognizes and receives divine nourishment. Let us trust Jesus, who fills us with His Spirit, and hold fast to Him in love and obedience. Let us look to Him to know the full meaning of the baptism of the Spirit in our lives.

And let us remember: He who is faithful in the least will be made ruler over much. Be faithful to what you already have and know of the Spirit's working. Regard yourself with deep reverence as God's holy temple. Wait for and listen to the gentlest whisper of God's Spirit within you. Listen particularly to the conscience that has been cleansed in the blood. Keep it clean by simple, childlike obedience. In your heart there may be involuntary sin over which you feel powerless. It is the root of selfishness that must be brought to the cross. Bring every sin to be cleansed in the blood.

With regard to your voluntary actions, day by day say to the Lord Jesus that everything you know to be pleasing to Him you will do. Yield to the reproofs of conscience when you fail; but come again, have hope in God, and renew your vow: What I know God wants me to do, I will do. Ask humbly every morning and wait for guidance; you will come to know the Spirit's voice, and you will know His strength and power to overcome. Jesus had His disciples three years in His baptism class, and then the blessing came. Be His loving, obedient disciple and believe in Him on whom the Spirit rested. Then you, too, shall be prepared for the fullness of the blessing of the baptism of the Spirit.

Blessed Lord Jesus! with my whole heart I worship you, as exalted on the throne to baptize with the Holy Spirit. Oh, reveal yourself to me in this your glory that I might know what I may expect from you.

I bless you that in yourself I have seen the preparation for receiving the Holy Spirit in His fullness. Even in your work in Nazareth, the Spirit was always with you. And yet when you surrendered yourself to fulfill all righteousness and to enter into fellowship with the sinners you came to save, in partaking of their baptism, you received from the Father a new inflowing of His Holy Spirit. It was to you the seal of His love, the revelation of His indwelling, and the power for service. And now you, on whom we see the Spirit descend and abide, do for us what the Father did for you.

Lord, I bless you that the Holy Spirit is in me, too. But I ask you to give me yet the full, overflowing measure you have promised. Let Him be to me the unceasing revelation of your presence in my heart as glorious and as mighty as on the throne of heaven. Lord Jesus, baptize me with the Holy Spirit. Amen.

Summary

1. All divine giving and working is in the power of an endless life. And so we can look up to Jesus each day, the blessed Light of this world: He baptizes with the Holy Spirit. He cleanses with the blood and baptizes with the Spirit according to each new need.

2. Let us keep inseparably connected in our faith the double truth John the Baptist preached: Jesus the Lamb takes away sin, Jesus the anointed baptizes with the Spirit. It was only in virtue of His shedding His blood that He

received the Spirit to pass on to us. It is as the cross is preached that the Spirit works. It is as I believe in the precious blood that cleanses from all sin, and walk before God with a conscience sprinkled with the blood, that I may claim the anointing of the Spirit. The blood and the oil go together. I need both. I have them both in Jesus, the Lamb on the throne.

Chapter 3

Worship in the Spirit

But the hour is coming, and now is, when the true worshipers will worship the Father in spirit and truth; for the Father is seeking such to worship Him. God is Spirit, and those who worship Him must worship in spirit and truth.

John 4:23–24

For we are the circumcision, who worship God in the Spirit, rejoice in Christ Jesus, and have no confidence in the flesh.

Philippians 3:3

To worship is man's highest glory. He was created for fellowship with God and of that fellowship worship is the greatest expression. All the exercises of the Christian life—meditation and prayer, love and faith, surrender and obedience—culminate in worship. Recognizing what God is in His holiness, His glory, and His love, realizing what I am as a sinful creature and as the Father's redeemed child, in worship I gather my being and present it to God. I offer Him the adoration and the glory that is due Him. The truest, fullest, and nearest approach to God is worship. Every sentiment and every service of the Christian life is included in it: To worship is man's highest destiny because in it God is all.

Jesus tells us that with His coming a new worship will commence. All that the heathen or the Samaritans called worship, all that even the Jews had known of worship, in accordance with the provisional revelation of God's law, would make way for something entirely and distinctively new—worship in spirit and in truth. This is the worship He was to inaugurate by giving us His Holy Spirit. This is the worship that now alone is well-pleasing to the Father. It is for this worship in particular that we have received the Holy Spirit. Let us at the very commencement of our study of the work of the Spirit embrace the blessed thought that the great purpose for which the Holy Spirit is within us is that we might worship in spirit and in truth. "For the Father is seeking such to worship him" (John 4:23). For this purpose He sent His Son and His Spirit.

In spirit. When God created man a living soul, that soul, as the seat and organ of his personality and consciousness, was linked on the one side, through the body, with the outer visible world, and on the other side, through the spirit, with the unseen and the divine. The soul had to decide whether it would yield itself to the spirit and by it to be linked with God and His will, or to the body and the solicitations of the visible. In the fall, the soul refused the rule of the spirit and became the slave of the body with its earthly appetites. Man became flesh; the spirit lost its destined place of rule and became little more than a dormant power. It was now no longer the ruling principle, but a struggling captive. And the spirit now stands in opposition to the *flesh* (the word for the life of the soul and body together) in its subjection to sin.

When speaking of the unregenerate man in contrast with the spiritual (1 Corinthians 2:14), Paul calls him the natural man. The life of the soul comprehends all our moral and intellectual faculties; they may even be directed toward the things of God, apart from the renewal of the divine Spirit. Because the soul is under the power of the flesh, man is spoken of as having *become* flesh, as being flesh. As the body consists of flesh and bone, and the flesh is that part that is especially endowed with sensitivity, and through which we receive sensations from the outer world, the flesh denotes human nature. It has become subject to the world of sense, or feeling. And because the soul has thus come under the power of the flesh, the Scripture speaks of all the attributes of the soul as belonging to the flesh and being under its power. So it contrasts, in reference to our practice of Christianity and worship, the two principles from which they may proceed. There is a fleshly wisdom and a spiritual wisdom (1 Corinthians 2:12). There is a service to God, trusting in the flesh and glorying in the flesh, and a service to God by the spirit (Philippians 3:3–4). There is a fleshly mind and a spiritual mind. There is a worship that is satisfying to the flesh, because it is in the power of what the flesh can do, and a worship of God that is in the spirit. It is this worship Jesus came to make possible and to realize in us, by giving a new spirit in our inmost being, and then within that, God's Holy Spirit.

Worship in spirit is worship in truth. Just as the words *in spirit* do not mean internal as contrasted with external observances, but spiritual, worked in us by God's Spirit (as opposed to what man's natural power can effect), so the words *in truth* do not mean sincere and upright. In all the worship of the Old Testament saints, they knew that God sought truth in the inward parts; they sought Him with their whole hearts, and yet they did not attain to that worship in spirit and truth that Jesus made possible when He rent the veil of the flesh. *Truth* here means the substance, the reality, the actual possession of all that the worship of God implies, both in what it demands and what it promises. John speaks of Jesus as "the only begotten of the Father, full of grace and truth" (John 1:14). And he adds, "For the law was given through Moses, but grace and truth came through Jesus Christ" (v. 17). If we compare truth to falsehood, the law of Moses was just as true as the gospel of Jesus; they both came from God. But the law was only a shadow of good things to come; Christ himself was the substance of those good things because He was himself the truth, the reality of God imparting itself to us. And so only worship *in spirit* is worship *in truth*, true enjoyment of the divine power that is Christ's own life and fellowship with the Father, revealed and maintained within us by the Holy Spirit.

True worshipers worship the Father in spirit and in truth. All who worship are not *true* worshipers. There may be a great deal of earnest, honest worship without it being worship that is in spirit and in truth. The mind might be intensely occupied, the feelings deeply moved, the will strongly stirred, and yet there might be at the same time very little spiritual worship that stands on the truth of God. There may be a great connection with Bible truth, and yet if the predominating activity of that one's worship stems from his or her own effort, it may not be the Spirit-breathed worship that God seeks of us. There must be true harmony between God, who is Spirit, and the worshiper who draws near in spirit. The infinite Holy Spirit, the true expression of God the Father, must be reflected in the spirit of the child. And this can only be as the Spirit of God dwells in us.

If we would become worshipers in spirit and in truth, the first thing we need to realize is the danger of worshiping in the flesh. As believers, we have in us a dual nature—flesh and spirit. The one is the natural part, ever ready to exalt itself and to undertake to do what is needed in the worship of God. The other is the spiritual part, which, if weak, the flesh will not allow it full control in the act of worship. Our minds may delight in the study of God's Word, we may even be moved by the thoughts it provokes, but we may yet be impotent to obey the law, to render the obedience and worship we would like (Romans 7:22–23).

We need the Holy Spirit's indwelling for life and worship. To receive Him fully, the flesh must be silenced. "Be silent, all flesh, before the Lord" (Zechariah 2:13). To Peter it had already been revealed that Jesus was the Christ, and yet he did not savor the thought of the cross. His mind was not in tune to the things of God but to the things of men. Our own thoughts of divine things, our own efforts to work up the right feelings, must be given up; our own power to worship must be seen for what it is: insufficient. Every approach to God must take place under a very distinct and quiet surrender to the Holy Spirit. As we learn how impossible it is to willfully ensure the Spirit's working, we will also learn that if we would worship in the Spirit we must walk in the Spirit. "But you are not in the flesh but in the Spirit, if indeed the Spirit of God dwells in you" (Romans 8:9). As the Spirit dwells and rules in me, I can worship in the Spirit.

"But the hour is coming, and now is, when the true worshipers will worship the Father in spirit and truth; for the Father is seeking such to worship Him" (John 4:23). Yes, the Father seeks such worshipers, and what He seeks He finds, because He himself calls us out. In order that we might be such worshipers, He sent His own Son to seek and to save the lost, that we should become His true worshipers, who enter in through the rent veil of the flesh and worship Him in the Spirit. When He sent the Spirit of His Son, He was the expression of the truth and reality of who Christ had been on earth. His actual presence will communicate within us the very life that Christ lived. The hour has come and now is; we are living in the moment when Christ's true worshipers can worship the Father in spirit and in truth. Let us believe it; the Spirit has been given and dwells within us for this reason: The Father seeks true worshipers. Let us rejoice in the confidence that we can attain to it because the Holy Spirit has been given.

Let us realize in holy fear and awe that He dwells within us. Let us humbly, in the silence of the flesh, yield ourselves to His leading and teaching. Let us wait in faith before God for His working. Let every new insight into what the work of the Spirit means, every exercise of faith in His indwelling or experience of His working, terminate in the adoring worship of the Father, giving Him the praise, thanks, honor, and love that belong to Him alone.

O God! You alone are Spirit, and they that worship you must worship in spirit and in truth. You sent your own Son to redeem and prepare us for this worship. You sent your Spirit to dwell in us and equip us for it. And now we have access to the Father, as through the Son, so in the Spirit.

We confess with shame how much of our worship has been in the power and the will of the flesh. By this we have dishonored you, grieved your Spirit, and brought infinite loss to our own souls. Forgive us, O God, and save us from this sin. Teach us, we pray, never to attempt to worship you by our own will and way, but in spirit and in truth.

Your Holy Spirit dwells in us. According to the riches of your glory, strengthen us with might by Him so that our inner man may be the spiritual temple you desire, where spiritual sacrifices are offered. Teach us the blessed art, as often as we enter your presence, of silencing self and flesh and waiting for the Spirit, who is in us, to aid us in true worship, seeking a faith and love that is acceptable to you, through Christ Jesus. May your church universal render you worship in spirit and in truth day by day. We ask it in the name of Jesus. Amen.

Summary

1. It is in worship that the Holy Spirit most thoroughly attains the purpose for which He was given; it is in worship that He can fully prove who He is. If we want the consciousness and the power of the Spirit's presence to become strong in us, we must worship. The Spirit equips us for worship: worship equips us for the Spirit.

2. It is not only prayer that is worship. Worship is the prostrate adoration of His holy presence. Often without words "the people bowed their heads and worshiped"

(Exodus 12:27; Nehemiah 8:6). "The twenty-four elders fell down and worshiped Him who lives forever and ever" (Revelation 5:14). Sometimes their worship was simply "Amen! Alleluia!" (Revelation 19:4).

3. There is so much worship—even among believers—that is not from our spirit, much less in the Spirit. In private, family, and public worship, there is so much hasty entering into God's presence in the power of the flesh with little or no waiting for the Spirit to lift us heavenward! It is only the presence and power of the Holy Spirit that equips us for acceptable worship.

4. The great hindrance to our own spirit is the flesh. The secret of spiritual worship is to silence the flesh, submitting it to the death of the cross. Aware of the flesh's action and ability to imitate, we must humbly wait for the Spirit's life and power to take the place of flesh and self.

5. As our life is, so will our worship be. The Spirit must lead and rule in daily life if He is to inspire our worship. A life in obedience to God's will and lived in His presence enables us to worship aright. May God convict us of the sinfulness and ineffectiveness of worship that is not in spirit and in truth.

6. The Spirit is given for worship. In an attitude of worship, let us humbly and reverently wait upon God.

The Spirit
and the Word

It is the Spirit who gives life; the flesh profits nothing.
The words that I speak to you are spirit, and they are life.
"Lord, to whom shall we go? You have the
words of eternal life."

John 6:63, 68

Who also made us sufficient as ministers of the new
covenant, not of the letter but of the Spirit; for
the letter kills, but the Spirit gives life.

2 Corinthians 3:6

Our blessed Lord has been speaking of himself as the bread
of life, and of His flesh and blood as the meat and drink of
eternal life. To many of His disciples it was a hard saying
that they could not understand. Jesus tells them that it is
only when the Holy Spirit is come, and they have Him, that
His words will become clear to them. He says, "It is the
Spirit who gives life; the flesh profits nothing."

In these words and in the corresponding ones of Paul, we have the nearest approach to what may be called a definition of the Spirit. (See 1 Corinthians 15:45, "a life-giving spirit.") The Spirit always acts, in the first place, whether in nature or grace, as a life-giving principle. It is of deepest importance to keep a firm grip on this. His work in the believer—sealing, sanctifying, enlightening, and strengthening—is rooted in this: It is as He is known and honored and place given to Him; as He is waited on as the inner life of the soul, that His other gracious workings are experienced. These are outgrowths of the inner life; it is in the power of the life within that they can be enjoyed. "It is the Spirit who gives life." In contrast, our Lord said: "The flesh profits nothing." He is not speaking here of the flesh as the foundation of sin. In its spiritual aspect, the flesh is the power in which the natural man, or even the believer who is not fully yielded to the Spirit, seeks to serve God or to know and grasp spiritual things. The futile character of all its efforts is indicated in the description "profits nothing." Its efforts are simply not sufficient; they do not avail us in reaching spiritual reality. Paul means the same when he says the letter kills. The whole dispensation of the law was but a dispensation of the letter and the flesh. Though it had a certain glory and Israel's privileges were very great, yet, as Paul says, "For even what was made glorious had no glory in this respect, because of the glory that excels" (2 Corinthians 3:10). Even Christ himself, as long as He was in the flesh, and until the dispensation of the Spirit took place, could not by His words effect in His disciples what He desired.

"The words that I speak to you are spirit, and they are

life" (John 6:63). He would teach the disciples two things. First, that words are living seeds with power to germinate, to spring up, asserting their own vitality, revealing their nature, and proving their power in those who receive them and keep them in their heart. He did not want them to be discouraged if they could not comprehend everything at once. His words are spirit and life; they are not meant only for understanding but for life itself. Coming in the power of the Spirit, higher and deeper than all thought, they enter into the very roots of our life. They have in themselves a divine life working out with a divine energy the truth they express into the experience of those who receive them. Second, as a consequence of this, His words need a spiritual nature to receive them. Seeds need a congenial soil: There must be life in the soil as well as in the seed. Not into the mind only, or into the feelings, or even into the will alone, but the Word must be taken through these avenues into the life. The center of that life is our spiritual nature, with conscience as its voice; there the authority of the Word must be acknowledged. But even this is not enough: The conscience dwells in man as a captive amid powers it cannot control. It is the Spirit that comes from God, the Spirit that brings life, and through the Word assimilates truth and power in us.

In our study of the work of the Holy Spirit, we cannot be too diligent at gaining a firm hold on this truth. It will save us from error. It will keep us from expecting to enjoy the teaching of the Spirit without the Word or to master the teaching of the Word without the Spirit.

In the Holy Trinity, the Word and the Spirit are intertwined—one with the Father. It is no different with the

God-inspired words of Scripture. The Holy Spirit has for all ages embodied the thoughts of God in the written Word, and lives now for this very purpose in our hearts—to reveal the power and the meaning of that Word. If you would be full of the Spirit, be full of the Word. If you would have the divine life of the Spirit within you grow strong in every part of your nature, let the word of Christ dwell in you richly. If you would have the Spirit fulfill His office of bringing to mind at the right moment and applying with divine accuracy what Jesus has spoken to your need, allow the words of Christ to abide in you. If you would have the Spirit reveal to you the will of God in each circumstance of life, choosing what you must do from conflicting commands or principles with unerring precision, suggesting His will as you need it, have the Word living in you, ready for His use. If you would have the eternal Word as your light, let the written Word be transcribed on your heart by the Holy Spirit. "The words that I speak to you are spirit, and they are life." Take them and treasure them: It is through them that the Spirit manifests His life-giving power.

Compare carefully Ephesians 5:18–19 and Colossians 3:16, and see how the joyful fellowship of the Christian life, described in the same words, is said in the one place to come from being full of the Spirit and in the other from being full of the Word.

Think not for one moment that the Word can unfold its life in you, except as the Spirit within you accepts and appropriates it in the inner life. How much of Scripture reading, study of Scripture, and scriptural preaching has as its primary goal arriving at the true meaning of the Word? Many think that if they know exactly what it means, the natural consequence will be the blessing that Word was intended to bring. This is not the case. The Word is a seed. In every seed there is a part in which the life is hidden. One may have the most perfect seed in substance, yet unless it is exposed in suitable soil to the influence of sun and moisture, it may never some to life. We may understand the words and doctrines of Scripture with our intellect and yet know little of their life or power. We need to remind ourselves and the church that the Scriptures spoken by holy men of old as they were moved by the Holy Spirit can only be understood by holy men as they are taught by the same Spirit.

This is one of the serious lessons that the history of the Jews in the time of Christ teaches us. They were exceedingly zealous, as they thought, for God's Word and honor and yet it turned out that all their zeal was for their human interpretation of God's Word. Jesus said to them: "You search the Scriptures, for in them you think you have eternal life; and these are they which testify of Me. But you are not willing to come to Me that you may have life" (John 5:39). They did indeed trust the Scriptures to lead them to eternal life, and yet they never saw that those words testified of Christ and so they would not come to Him. They studied and accepted Scripture in the light and power of their human reasoning and understanding rather than in the light and power of God's Spirit as their life.

The weakness in the life of so many believers who read and know considerable Scripture is because they do not know that it is the Spirit that gives life, and that the flesh— human understanding, however intelligent, however earnest—profits nothing. They think that in the Scriptures they have eternal life. But they know little of the living Christ in the power of the Spirit as their true life.

What is needed is very simple: the determined refusal to attempt to interpret the written Word without the life-giving Spirit. Let us never take Scripture into our hand, mind, or mouth, without realizing the need and the promise of the Spirit. First, in an act of quiet faith, look to God to give and renew the workings of His Spirit within you. Then yield yourself to the power that dwells within you, and wait on Him so that not the mind alone but the life in you may be opened to receive the Word.

As we further follow the teaching of our blessed Lord with regard to the Spirit, it will become clear to us that as the Lord's words are spirit and life, so the Spirit must be in us as the spirit of our life. Our inmost personal life must reflect the Spirit of God. Deeper than mind, feeling, or will—the very root of all these and their motivating principle—there must be the Spirit of God. If we seek to go beyond these faculties, we find that nothing equals the Spirit of life in the words of the living God. If we wait on the Holy Spirit, in the depths of our soul, to reveal the words by His life-giving power and apply them to our life, we will know in truth what the word means: "It is the Spirit that gives life."

O my God, again I thank you for the wonderful gift of the indwelling Spirit. And I humbly ask you afresh that I may truly know that He is in me and how glorious is the divine work He is doing.

Teach me especially, I pray, to believe that He is the life and strength of the growth of divine life within me, the pledge and assurance that I can grow up into all you would have me be. As I see this, I will more fully understand how the Spirit of life within me can make my spirit hunger for the Word as the bread of life.

Forgive me, Lord, when I have sought to comprehend your words in the power of my own intellect. I have been slow to learn that the flesh profits nothing. I do desire to learn it now.

Give me, Father, the spirit of wisdom to interpret each word of yours and to remember that spiritual things can only be spiritually discerned. Teach me in all my interaction with your Word to deny the flesh, to wait in humility and faith for the inward working of the Spirit to quicken your Word to my heart. Likewise, in all my meditation of your Word, may I keep it in faith and obedience. Amen.

Summary

1. To understand a book, the reader must speak the same language as the author. He must in many cases have somewhat of the same spirit in which the author wrote the book. To understand the Scripture, we need the same Holy Spirit dwelling in us that enabled men of old to write it.

2. The eternal Word and the eternal Spirit are inseparable. So are the creative word and the creative Spirit (Genesis 1:2–3; Psalm 33:6). The Word and the Spirit work together in redemption (John 1:1–3, 14). In the written Word: "The words that I speak to you are spirit." So the word preached by the apostles was in the power of the Spirit (1 Thessalonians 1:5). As we read and meditate on God's Word, we must depend upon the Holy Spirit to interpret it to our hearts.

3. The Word is a seed. The seed has a hidden life that needs a living soil in which to germinate and grow. The Word has a divine life; see that you receive the Word not only in the natural mind or will but in your new spirit, where God's Spirit dwells.

4. The power of the Word and its truth depend upon living fellowship with Jesus. Why is there so often failure instead of victory in the Christian life? It is because the truth is held apart from the power of the Spirit. May God help me to believe these two things: the Word is full of divine Spirit and power and can work mightily; the heart has the same divine Spirit, through whom the living Word is accepted in living power. My life must be directed in the power of the Spirit.

Chapter 5

The Spirit of the Glorified Jesus

He who believes in Me, as the Scripture has said, out of his heart will flow rivers of living water. But this He spoke concerning the Spirit, whom those believing in Him would receive; for the Holy Spirit was not yet given, because Jesus was not yet glorified.

John 7:38–39

Our Lord promises here that those who come unto Him and drink, who believe in Him, will not only never thirst, but will themselves become fountains from which will flow streams of living water of life and blessing. In recording the words, John explains that the promise was a prospective one that would have to wait for its fulfillment—when the Holy Spirit would be poured out. He also gave the double reason for this delay: "The Holy Spirit was not yet given, because Jesus was not yet glorified." The original expression "the Spirit was not yet" appeared strange, so the word *given* was inserted. But the expression, accepted as it stands, may guide us into the true understanding of the significance of the Spirit's not coming until Jesus was glorified.

We have seen that God has given a twofold revelation of himself—first as God in the Old Testament, then as Father in the New. We know how the Son, who had from eternity been with the Father, entered upon a new stage of existence when He became flesh. When He returned to heaven, He was still the same only-begotten Son of God and yet not altogether the same. For He was now also the first-begotten from the dead, clothed with the glorified humanity that He had perfected and sanctified. Likewise, the Spirit of God poured out at Pentecost was indeed something new. Through the Old Testament He was always called the Spirit of God or the Spirit of the Lord; the name HOLY SPIRIT was not yet used as His proper name. The only passages in the Old Testament where we have in our translation *Holy Spirit*, the Hebrew is properly *the Spirit of His holiness* (Psalm 51:11; Isaiah 63:10–11). The word is used of the Spirit of God and not as the proper name of the third person of the Trinity. Only in the New Testament does the Spirit bear the name *Holy Spirit*. It is only in connection with the work He has to do in preparing the way for Christ, and a body for Him, that the proper name comes into use (Luke 1:15, 35). When poured out at Pentecost, He came as the Spirit of the glorified Jesus, the Spirit of the incarnate, crucified, and exalted Christ, the bearer and communicator to us not of the life of God as such, but of that life as it had been interwoven into human nature in the person of Christ Jesus. It is particularly in this capacity that He bears the name *Holy Spirit*, for it is as the indwelling one that God is holy.

Of this Spirit, as He dwelt in Jesus in the flesh and can dwell in us in the flesh, too, it is distinctly and literally true: The Holy Spirit was not yet. The Spirit of the glorified Jesus—the Son of man become the Son of God—could not *be* until Jesus was glorified.

This thought further opens up to us the reason why it is not the Spirit of God as such but the Spirit of Jesus that was sent to dwell in us. Sin had not only disturbed our relationship to God's law but to God himself; with the divine favor we lost the divine life. Christ came not only to deliver us from the law and its curse, but to bring human nature back into fellowship with the divine life, to make us partakers of the divine nature. He could not do this by an exercise of divine power on humankind, but only through a free moral agent. In His own person, having become flesh, He sanctified the flesh and made it a fit and willing receptacle for the indwelling of the Spirit of God. Having done this, He had, in death (in accordance with the law that the lower form of life can rise to a higher only through decay and death), both to bear the curse of sin and to give himself as the seed to bring forth fruit in us. From His nature, as it was glorified in the resurrection and ascension, His Spirit came forth as the spirit of His human life, glorified into union with the divine, to make us partakers of all that He had personally worked out and acquired of himself and His glorified life. By virtue of His atonement, man now had a right and title to the fullness of the divine Spirit and to His indwelling as never before.

And by His having perfected in himself a new, holy, human nature on our behalf, He could now communicate what previously did not exist—a life both human and divine. From henceforth the Spirit, just as He was the personal divine life, could also become the personal life of humankind. Even as the Spirit is the personal life principle in God himself, so He can be in the child of God: the Spirit of God's Son can now be the Spirit that cries with our heart, "Abba, Father." Of this Spirit it is most true: "The Holy Spirit was not yet, because Jesus was not yet glorified."

But now, praise God, Jesus has been glorified; we have the Spirit of the glorified Jesus; the promise of our text can now be fulfilled: "He who believes in Me, as the Scripture has said, out of his heart will flow rivers of living water." The great transaction that took place when Jesus was glorified is now an eternal reality. He first entered into our human nature, our flesh, and after having given himself over to death for us, He stood at the right hand of God. Then that of which Peter spoke took place: "Being exalted to the right hand of God, and having received from the Father the promise of the Holy Spirit, He poured out this which you now see and hear" (Acts 2:33). In our place and on our behalf, as man and the head of humankind, He was admitted into the full glory of the divine, and His human nature constituted the receptacle and the dispenser of the divine Spirit. The Holy Spirit descended as the Spirit of the God-man—actually the Spirit of God, and yet as truly the spirit of man. He is the Spirit of the glorified Jesus, come to dwell in each one who believes in Jesus, the Spirit of His personal life and presence while at the same time the spirit of the personal life of the believer. Just as in Jesus the perfect union of God and man was accomplished, and then completed when He sat down on the throne and so entered a new stage of existence, a glory before unknown, now also a new era has begun in the life and work of the Spirit. He now witnesses the perfect union of the divine and the human. In becoming our life, He makes us partakers of it. There is *now* the Spirit of the glorified Jesus: He has been poured out, we have received Him. He flows through us and from us in rivers of blessing.

The glorifying of Jesus and the pouring forth of His Spirit are intimately connected; in vital organic union the two are inseparably linked. If we would have not only the Spirit of God but also the Spirit of Christ, who "was not yet" but now is, the Spirit of the glorified Jesus, it is with the glorified Jesus we must deal by faith. We cannot rest with the faith that trusts in the cross and its pardon; we must go on to know the new life, the life of glory and power divine in human nature, of which the Spirit of the glorified Jesus is the witness and the bearer. This is the mystery hid from generations past, but now is made known by the Holy Spirit, *Christ in us:* He can actually live His divine life in us and through us who are in the flesh. We have the most intense personal interest in knowing and understanding what it means that Jesus is glorified, that human nature shares the life and glory of God. It is important that we understand this not only because we will one day see Him in His glory and share in it, but even *now,* day by day, we are to live in it. The Holy Spirit is able to *be* to us as much as we are willing to *have* of Him.

God be praised! Jesus has been glorified. We have the Spirit of the glorified Jesus. In the Old Testament only the unity of God was revealed; when the Spirit was mentioned, it was always as His Spirit, the power by which God was working. He was not yet known on earth as a person. In the New Testament, the Trinity is revealed; on Pentecost the Holy Spirit descended as a person to dwell in us. This is the fruit of Jesus' work—that we can have the personal presence of the Holy Spirit on earth. In Christ Jesus, the second person, the Son came to reveal the Father, and the Father dwelt in and spoke through Him. Likewise, the Spirit, the third person, comes to reveal the Son, and in Him the Son dwells and works in us. This is the glory wherewith the Father glorified the Son of man, because the Son glorified Him. In His name and through Him, the Holy Spirit descends as a person to dwell in believers and to make the glorified Jesus a present reality. It is He of whom Jesus spoke when He said that whoever believes in Him will never thirst but will have rivers of living waters flowing out of him. This alone satisfies the soul's thirst, making it a fountain that gives life to others—the personal indwelling of the Holy Spirit, revealing the presence of the glorified Jesus.

"He who believes in Me . . . out of his heart will flow rivers of living water." Once again, the key to all God's treasures is to believe in Him. It is the glorified Jesus who baptizes with the Holy Spirit. Everyone who longs for the full blessing here promised must only believe. According to the riches of His glory, God works in us. He has given His Holy Spirit so that we have His personal presence on earth and within us. By faith the glory of Jesus in heaven and the power of the Spirit in our hearts become inseparably linked. Faith is the power of the renewed nature that forsakes self and makes room for the glorified Christ. By faith in Jesus, bow in quiet surrender before Him, fully assured that as you wait on Him, the river will flow.

Blessed Lord Jesus! I do believe; help my unbelief. As author and perfecter of our faith, perfect the work of faith in me. Teach me, I pray, with a faith that enters the unseen to realize what your glory is and what my share in it is even now, according to your Word: "The glory you gave me, I have given them." Teach me that the Holy Spirit and His power is the glory that you give us, and that you would have us show forth your glory, rejoicing in His holy presence on earth and His indwelling in us. Teach me above all, blessed Lord, not only to hold these blessed truths in my mind, but with my inmost spirit to wait on you to be filled with your Spirit.

Glorified Lord! I do even now bow before your glory in humble faith. Let all the life of self and the flesh be abased and perish as I worship and wait before you. Let the Spirit of glory become my life. Let His presence break down all confidence in self and make room for you. Let my whole life be one of faith in the Son of God, who loved me and gave himself for me. Amen.

Summary

1. In Christ there was an outward lowly state as Servant that preceded His state of glory as King. It was His faithfulness in the first that led Him to the second. Let every believer who longs to partake with Christ in His glory, first faithfully follow Him in His denial of self; the Spirit will in due time reveal the glory within Him.

2. Christ's glory was particularly the fruit of His suffering—the death of the cross. It is as I enter into the death of the cross in its double aspect—Christ being crucified for me, my being crucified with Christ—that the heart is opened for the Spirit's revelation of the glorified Christ.

3. It is not only in having wonderful thoughts and visions of my Lord's glory that satisfies me, it is *Christ himself glorified in me,* in my personal life, by way of a divine and heavenly power uniting His life in glory with my life; it is this alone that can satisfy His heart and mine.

4. Again I say, glory to God! This Spirit, the Spirit of the glorified One, is within me. He has possession of my inmost life. By His grace I will draw that life away from the ways of self and sin, and wait and worship in the assured confidence that He will take full possession of me and will glorify the Lord through me.

Chapter 6

The Indwelling Spirit

And I will pray the Father, and He will give you another
Helper, that He may abide with you forever; the Spirit of
truth, whom the world cannot receive, because it neither
sees Him nor knows Him; but you know Him, for He
dwells with you and will be in you.

John 14:16–17

"He . . . will be in you." In these simple words our Lord announces that wonderful mystery of the Spirit's indwelling that was to be the fruit and the crown of His redeeming work. It was for this that man was created. It was for this— God's mastery of the human heart—that the Spirit labored in vain through ages past. It was for this Jesus lived and died. Without the indwelling Spirit, the Father's purpose and work would not have been accomplished. For lack of it the blessed Master's work with the disciples had little effect. He hardly mentioned it to them because He knew they would not understand it. But on the last night, when time was running out, He disclosed the secret that when He left them, their loss would be compensated by a greater blessing than His bodily presence could accomplish. Another would come in His place to abide with them forever.

Our Father has given us a twofold revelation of himself. Through His Son He reveals *His holy image*, and setting Him before us invites us to become like Him by receiving Him into our heart and life. Through His Spirit He sends His divine power to enter into us and from within prepare us for receiving the Son and the Father. The dispensation of the Spirit is the dispensation of the inner life. The dispensation of the Word, or the Son, began with the creation of man in God's image and continued through all the preparatory stages down to Christ's appearing in the flesh. There were, at times, special and mighty workings of the Spirit, but the indwelling was unknown; humankind had not yet become a habitation of God in the Spirit. This was yet to be attained. Eternal life would become the life of man, infusing his being and consciousness and clothing itself in the forms of a human will and life. Just as it is through the Spirit that God is what He is, and as the Spirit is the principle by which the personalities of the Father and the Son have their root and consciousness, likewise this Spirit of the divine life is to be *in us*. In the deepest sense of the word, He should be the principle of our life, the root of our personality, the very spark of our being and consciousness. He is to be one with us in the absoluteness of a divine immanence—dwelling in us, even as the Father is in the Son and the Son is in the Father. Let us bow in holy reverence to worship and adore Him and to receive this blessing.

If we would enter into the full understanding and experience of what our blessed Lord here promises, we must, above everything, remember that what He speaks of is a *divine* indwelling. Wherever God dwells He hides himself. He dwells in nature, but many do not see Him there. In meeting His saints of old He usually concealed himself under some manifestation in human weakness so that it was often only after He was gone that they said, "Surely the Lord is in this place, and we knew it not." In the tabernacle and the temple God dwelt in the darkness; He was there, but behind a veil, to be believed in and feared, but not to be seen. The Son came to reveal God, and yet He came as a root out of dry ground, without form or comeliness; even His own disciples were at times offended by Him. People expect the kingdom of God to come with observation. They do not know that it is a hidden mystery to be received only as, in His own self-revealing power, God makes himself known in hearts surrendered and prepared for Him. When contemplating the promise of the Spirit, Christians want some idea as to how His leading is known in their thoughts; how His quickening affects their feelings; how His sanctifying can be recognized in their will and conduct. They need to be reminded that deeper than mind, feeling, and will, deeper than the soul, where these have their seat, in the depths of the spirit that came from God, there the Holy Spirit comes to dwell.

This indwelling is to be, first of all, recognized by faith. Even when I cannot see the smallest evidence of His working, I am to believe that He dwells in me. In that faith I am to rest and trust His working, and to wait for it. I also must purposefully set aside my own wisdom and strength and in childlike self-denial depend upon Him to work. His first stirrings may be so quiet and hidden that I can hardly recognize them as coming from Him; they may appear to be nothing more than the voice of conscience or the familiar sound of some Bible truth. This is the time when by faith we must hold fast to the Master's promise and the Father's gift and to trust that the Spirit is within and will guide us. By faith we must continually yield our whole being to His rule and mastery and be faithful to what appears the nearest to His voice until we come to know His voice better.

Faith is the faculty of our spiritual nature by which we can recognize the divine, in whatever unlikely appearance it clothes itself. If this is true of the Father in His glory as God, and of the Son as the manifestation of the Father, how much more must it be true of the Spirit, the unseen divine life-power come to clothe itself and conceal itself within our weakness? Let us cultivate and exercise our faith in the Father, whose gift through the Son is the Spirit in our hearts. Let us look in faith to the Son also, whose glory centers in the gift of the indwelling Spirit. Likewise, let our faith grow strong in the unseen, sometimes unfelt, divine presence of this mighty power. He is a living person, who has descended into our weakness and hidden himself in our smallness to equip us for becoming the dwelling of the Father and the Son. Let our adoring worship of our glorified Lord seek to grasp the wondrous answer He gives to every prayer as the seal of our acceptance. It is the promise of deeper knowledge of our God, of closer fellowship and richer blessedness: The Holy Spirit dwells in us.

The deep importance of a right apprehension of the indwelling of the Spirit is evident from the place it occupies in our Lord's farewell discourse. In this and the two following chapters, He speaks of the Spirit more directly as a teacher and witness, as representing and glorifying himself, and as convincing the world. At the same time, He connects what He says of His and the Father's indwelling, of the union of the vine and the branches, and of the peace and joy and power in prayer that His disciples would have with "that day"—the time of the Spirit's coming. But before all this, as its one condition and only source, He places the promise: "The Spirit of truth . . . will be in you." It is of no benefit to us if we know all that the Spirit can do for us, or that we confess our entire dependence upon Him, unless we clearly realize and put in proper perspective what the Master deems most important. It is as the indwelling Spirit alone that He can be our teacher and our strength. As the church, and each believer, accepts our Lord's promise "He will be in you" and takes this truth by faith, our relationship to the Holy Spirit will be restored. He will take control and inspire; He will fill and bless the vessel given over to Him as His dwelling.

A careful study of the epistles will confirm this. In writing to the Corinthians, Paul had to reprove them for sad and terrible sins and yet he says to all, including the weakest and most unfaithful believer, "Do you not know that you are the temple of God and that the Spirit of God dwells in you?" (1 Corinthians 3:16). He was certain that if this was truly believed, and the truth given the place God intended, it would not only be the motive but the power of a new life. He reminded the backsliding Galatians that they had received the Spirit by the preaching of faith; God had sent the Spirit of His Son into their hearts; they had their life by the Spirit in them; if they could but understand and believe it, they would also walk in the Spirit.

It is this teaching the church of Christ needs in our day. I am convinced that very few of us realize to what extent believers are ignorant of this aspect of the truth concerning the Holy Spirit or to what extent this is the cause of their lacking in holiness of walk and work. There may be regular prayer for the Holy Spirit's working; we may be honest in our confession of our need of Him, even of absolute dependence upon Him; but unless His personal, continual, divine indwelling is acknowledged and experienced, we cannot be too surprised if there is failure. The holy dove wants His resting-place free from all intrusion and disturbance. God wants entire possession of His temple. Jesus wants His home to himself. He cannot do His work, He cannot rule and reveal himself as He would, until the whole temple, the whole inner being, is possessed and filled with the Holy Spirit.

Let us consent to this. As the meaning of His indwelling dawns upon us in its full extent and claim, as we accept its divine reality, as we bow in emptiness and surrender, faith and adoration, the Father will for Jesus' sake delight to make it our experience. We will know that the secret and the power of the life of a true disciple is the indwelling Spirit.

Lord Jesus, my soul is blessed by your precious Word: The Spirit will be in you. In deep humility I once again accept it and ask you to teach me its full meaning.

I ask for myself and all God's children that we may understand how near and dear your love would come to us, how entirely and intimately you would give yourself to us if we would but allow your Spirit to dwell in us. Nothing can satisfy you fully but to have your residence within us, to dwell in us as our life. To this end you have sent your Holy Spirit into our hearts to be the power that lives and acts in our inmost being to give us the full revelation of yourself. Allow your church to see and know this truth that has been until now largely hidden, to experience it and to bear witness to it in power. May the joyful sound be heard throughout her borders, that every true believer has the indwelling and the leading of your Holy Spirit.

Teach me, Lord, the life of faith that goes beyond itself to wait on you, as by your Spirit you do your work within me. May my life from hour to hour bask in the holy, humble consciousness that Christ's Spirit dwells in me. Amen.

Summary

1. The coming of the Son of God in the likeness of sinful flesh, the Word being made flesh, and His dwelling in our nature is a true mystery! Great is the mystery of godliness! Great the mystery of the Spirit of God dwelling in us who are only sinful flesh!

2. There is an introspection in which the soul looks at its own thoughts, feelings, and purposes to find the proof of grace and the grounds of peace. This is not of faith, as it turns the eye from Christ to self. But there is another turning inward that is a noble exercise of faith. It is when the soul, closing the eye to all of self, seeks to realize in faith that there is a new spirit, within which the Spirit of Christ dwells. In this faith it unreservedly gives itself over to be renewed by the Spirit and yields

every faculty of the soul to be sanctified and guided by the Spirit within.

3. When entering a temple, the first thought is reverence. The first and abiding thought connected with the Spirit's dwelling in me as His temple is also a deep reverence and awe before His holy presence.

4. Hold fast to the thought of the permanence of His presence with the church, the intimacy of His presence in every believer.

— Chapter 7 —

The Spirit Is Given
to the Obedient

If you love Me, keep My commandments. . . .
And He will give you another Helper, that He
may abide with you forever.

John 14:15–16

And we are His witnesses to these things, and so also is
the Holy Spirit whom God has given to those who obey Him.

Acts 5:32

The expression of this truth suggests the question: How can this be? Don't we need the Spirit to make us obedient? We long for the Spirit's power because we regret the disobedience we find in ourselves, and we desire to be otherwise. But the Savior claims obedience as the condition of the Father's giving and our receiving the Spirit.

The dilemma is resolved if we remember that there is a twofold manifestation of the Spirit of God corresponding to the Old and New Testaments. In the former, He works as the Spirit of God preparing the way for the higher revelation of God, as the Father of Jesus Christ. In this way He worked in Christ's disciples as the Spirit of faith and conversion. What they were now about to receive was something higher—the Spirit of the glorified Jesus communicating the power from on high, the experience of His full salvation. Although now to all believers under the New Testament economy, the Spirit in them is the Spirit of Christ, there is still something that corresponds to the twofold dispensation. Where there is little knowledge of the Spirit's work or where His working in a church or an individual is weak, believers may not get beyond the experience of His preparatory work in them. Though He is in them, they may not know Him in His power as the Spirit of the glorified Lord. He is in them to make them obedient. It is only as they yield obedience to this His more elementary work, the keeping of Christ's commandments, that they will be promoted to the higher experience of His conscious indwelling.

The lesson is one we cannot study too closely. In the angels of heaven, in God's own Son, only by obedience could the relationship with the divine being be maintained and admission secured to a closer experience of His love and life. God's will revealed is the expression of His hidden perfection. Only in accepting and doing His will, to the giving up of our will to be possessed and used as He pleases, are we equipped to enter into His divine presence. It was so with the Son of God. It was after a life of humility and obedience, at thirty years of age, when He gave himself to the baptism of repentance, that He was baptized with the Spirit. The Spirit came because of His obedience. And it was after He had learned obedience in suffering and became obedient to the death of the cross that He again received the Spirit from the Father to pour out on His disciples: "Therefore being exalted to the right hand of God, and having received from the Father the promise of the Holy Spirit, He poured out this which you now see and hear" (Acts 2:33). The fullness of the Spirit for His body, the church, was the reward of obedience. This law of the Spirit's coming, as revealed in the Head, holds for every member of the body. Obedience is the indispensable condition of the Spirit's indwelling.

Christ Jesus came to prepare the way for the Spirit's coming. His outward coming in the flesh was the preparation for His inward coming in the Spirit. The outward coming appealed to the soul with its mind and feelings. It was only as Christ in His outward coming was accepted, as He was loved and obeyed, that the inward and more intimate revelation would be given. Personal attachment to Jesus, the personal acceptance of Him as Lord and Master to love and obey, was the disciples' preparation for the baptism of the Spirit. Even now, it is in listening to the voice of conscience and a faithful commitment to keep the commands of Jesus that we prove our love to Him and our hearts are prepared for the fullness of the Spirit. Our attainments may fall short of our goals; we may sometimes have to admit that what we would do we do not do. But if the Master sees our wholehearted surrender to His will and our faithful obedience to what we already have of the leading of His Spirit, we may be sure that the full gift will not be withheld.

These words suggest the two reasons why the presence

and the power of the Spirit in the church are often not realized. It is not always understood that although the obedience of love must precede the fullness of the Spirit, we must wait for the fullness to follow. Those who want the fullness of the Spirit before they obey err no less than those who think obedience is a sign that the fullness of the Spirit is already present.

Obedience must precede the baptism of the Spirit. John preached Jesus as the true baptizer—the one who would baptize with the Holy Spirit and with fire. Jesus took His disciples as candidates for this baptism into a three-year training course. First of all, He took them in as close friends in ministry. He taught them to forsake all for Him. He called himself their Master and Lord and taught them to do what He said. Then in His farewell discourse He spoke of obedience to His commands as the one condition for further spiritual blessing. I suspect the church has not given this word *obedience* the prominence that Christ gave it. Some of the reasons have been the danger of self-righteousness, exalting free grace, the power of sin, and the natural reluctance of the flesh to accept a high standard of holiness. While the freedom of grace and the simplicity of faith have been preached, the absolute necessity of obedience and holiness has not been equally presented. The general thought has been that only those who have the fullness of the Spirit can be obedient. Again, we must realize that obedience is the *first step*. The baptism of the Spirit, the full revelation of the glorified Lord working in us and through us follows as God's part. It is not understood in every sector that simple, full allegiance to every dictate of conscience and every precept of the Word is the passport to that full life in the Spirit.

As the natural consequence of the neglect of this truth, the companion truth is also forgotten: *The obedient must and may look for the fullness of the Spirit.* The promise to the obedient of the conscious, active indwelling of the Spirit is a fact unknown to many Christians. The greater part of life is spent in regret over disobedience, regret over a lack of the Spirit's power, and prayer for the Spirit to *help* us obey, instead of rising in the strength of the Spirit already in us to obedience as indeed possible and necessary. The fact that the Holy Spirit is sent to the obedient to give them the presence of Jesus as a continuous reality is scarcely thought of. The meaning of the life of Jesus as our example is not always understood. Jesus lived the outward lowly life of trial and obedience in preparation for the hidden spiritual life of power and glory. It is of this inner life that we are made partakers in the gift of the Spirit of the glorified Jesus. But in our inner personal participation of that gift, we must walk in the way He prepared for us. Through our putting to death the works of the flesh, we yield ourselves to God to do in us what He will and also that we do His will. We then experience God in His fullness. Accepting His will with the same heart with which He embraced it is the home of the Holy Spirit. The revelation of the Son in His perfect obedience was the condition of the outpouring of the Spirit; the acceptance of the Son in love and obedience is the path to the indwelling of the Spirit.

It is this truth that has in recent years been revealed with power to the hearts of many, described by the terms *full surrender* and *entire consecration.* As these have understood that the Lord Jesus claims implicit obedience and that the giving up of all to Him and His will is absolutely necessary, they have found entrance into a life of peace and strength previously unknown. Many are learning that they have not yet grasped it. They will find that there are applications of this principle beyond what they have conceived. As we understand how in the power of the Spirit, as we already possess Him in salvation, every part of our life can be brought into allegiance to Jesus, and as we give ourselves to it in faith, we will see that the Spirit of the glorified Lord can work His mighty work in us in a way far beyond what we could ask or think. God intended that the indwelling of the Holy Spirit be to the church more than it has yet known.

Let us ask God to awaken His church to grasp this double lesson: A living obedience is indispensable to the full experience of the indwelling; the full experience of the indwelling is what a loving obedience may claim. Let us say to our Lord that we love Him and desire to keep His commandments. However weak and faltering it may sound, let us speak it out to Him as the purpose of our souls. He will accept our commitment. Let us believe in the Spirit as already given to us, when in the obedience of faith we gave ourselves to Christ. And then let us believe that the full indwelling, with the revelation of Christ, can be ours also.

Blessed Lord, with my whole heart I accept the teaching of these words. And I ask that you will write the truth ever deeper on my heart as one of the laws of your kingdom, that loving obedience may look for a loving acceptance, sealed by an ever-increasing experience of the power of the Spirit.

I thank you for what your Word teaches of the love and obedience of your disciples. Though still imperfect—did they not all forsake you?—yet you covered their shortcomings with the cloak of your love. With my whole heart I say I love you and want to keep all of your commandments.

I surrender myself afresh to you for this purpose. In the depths of my soul you must see that there is but one desire: Your will be done in me as it is done in heaven.

To every reproof of conscience I would bow low; to every moving of your Spirit I would yield implicit obedience. I give my will and my life unto your death, that being raised with you, your Holy Spirit that dwells in me and reveals you to me may be my whole life. Amen.

Summary

1. When God commanded Israel to build a holy place that He might dwell among them, He told Moses to follow the pattern He had given, to make it as He commanded. It was in a house built after God's pattern, to His mind, the perfect expression of His will, that God came to dwell. In the will of God, carried out by man, God finds a home. God dwells in the obedience of His people.

2. In this house, the throne of God, He placed His mercy-seat and the ark in which were kept the tables of the law. In the new spirit, where God writes His law and where it is kept, there the Lord reveals His presence.

3. Before God came down to dwell with them, it cost Israel time and sacrifice to prepare a house for Him. If you pray for the revelation of Jesus, be sure your heart is prepared to be His temple. Does conscience testify that you

seek with your whole heart to know and do the will of the Lord?

4. It is only when God's will is accepted as our only law, and the commands of Jesus are by the Holy Spirit written in the heart, that the glory of God can fill His temple.

5. If you would know the indwelling of the Spirit as a blessed reality, let your conscience be kept pure, let your joy each day be in the testimony that your life has been an example of obedience to the Lord.

Chapter 8

Knowing the Spirit

The Spirit of truth, whom the world cannot receive,
because it neither sees Him nor knows Him; but you know
Him, for He dwells with you and will be in you.

John 14:17

Do you not know that you are the temple of God and that
the Spirit of God dwells in you?

1 Corinthians 3:16

The value of knowledge—true spiritual knowledge—in the life of faith can hardly be exaggerated. Just as a man on earth is none the richer for an inheritance that comes to him, or a treasure in his field, as long as he does not know of it or does not know how to gain possession of it and utilize it—so the gifts of God's grace cannot bring their full blessing until we know and, in knowing, truly apprehend them. "In [Christ] are hidden all the treasures of wisdom and knowledge" (Colossians 2:3). It is for the full *knowledge* of Christ Jesus his Lord that the believer is willing to count all things but loss. It is because of a lack of the true knowledge of what God in Christ has prepared for us that the lives of believers are so often weak. The prayer Paul offered for the Ephesians—that the Father would give them "the spirit of wisdom and revelation in the knowledge of Him," the eyes of their understanding being enlightened, that they might *know* "what is the hope of His calling, what are the riches of the glory of His inheritance in the saints, and what is the exceeding greatness of His power toward us who believe" (1:17–19)—is a prayer we never can offer enough, whether for ourselves or for others. But it is of particular importance that we know the teacher through whom all knowledge is to come! The Father has given each one of His children not only Christ, who is the truth, the reality of all life and grace, but the Holy Spirit, who is the very Spirit of Christ.

Some might ask: How do we know when it is the Spirit that is teaching us? We must know the teacher. It is only by knowing Him that we will be able to discern that our spiritual knowledge is genuine and not a deception. Our Lord meets this question, with all the solemn issues depending upon it, by assuring us that we shall *know* the Spirit. When a messenger comes to speak for a king or a witness gives testimony for a friend, neither speaks of himself, and yet without doing so each draws attention to himself and claims recognition of his presence and trustworthiness. So the Holy Spirit, when He testifies of Christ, must be known and acknowledged in His divine commission and presence. It is only then that we can have the assurance that the knowledge we receive is indeed of God and not something our human reasoning has gathered. To know the King's seal is the only safeguard against a counterfeit image. To know the Spirit is our foundation of certainty.

How can we know the Spirit in this way? Jesus says: "You know him, for he dwells with you and will be in you." The abiding indwelling of the Spirit is the condition of knowing Him. His presence will be self-evident. As we allow Him to dwell in us, giving Him full freedom in faith and obedience, and allowing Him to testify of Jesus as Lord, He will bring His credentials: He will prove himself to be the Spirit of God. It is because the presence of the Spirit as the indwelling teacher of every believer is so little acknowledged in the church, and therefore His manifestations few, that there is so much difficulty and hesitation about recognizing the witness of the Spirit. As the truth and experience of the indwelling of the Spirit are restored among God's people, and the Spirit is free again to work in power among us, His blessed presence will be its own proof.

Meanwhile, to everyone who honestly desires to know that he has the Spirit and to know Him in His person as a friend and teacher, we say, study the teaching of the Word with regard to the Spirit. Do not be content with the teaching of the church or of men, but go directly to His Word. If you are in earnest to know the Spirit, search the Word with this in view as one who thirsts to drink deeply of the water of life. Gather all that the Word says of the Spirit, His indwelling and His work, and guard it in your heart. Be determined to accept nothing but what the Word teaches and to accept it wholeheartedly.

If you are a child of God, you have the Spirit, even though you may not yet know how He manifests himself in you. Ask the Father to work through Him in you and to illuminate the Word to you. If in the spirit of humility and trusting in God's guidance, you submit heartily to the Word, you will find the promise fulfilled: You will be taught of God. We have spoken of the progress from the outward in: Be diligent in giving up your own thoughts and those of others as you accept the Word as revealed to you by His Spirit.

The primary signs by which the Spirit can be known to us are two. The first will be external—referring to the work He does. The second will be the inner life—the disposition of those in whom He dwells.

Just as loving obedience is the condition of the Spirit's coming, so it is the abiding mark of His presence. Jesus gave Him to us as teacher and guide. All Scripture speaks of His work as demanding the surrender of the whole life.

> For if you live according to the flesh you will die; but if by the Spirit you put to death the deeds of the body, you will live. For as many as are led by the Spirit of God, these are sons of God. . . . Your body is the temple of the Holy Spirit who is in you, whom you have from God, and you are not your own. For you were bought at a price; therefore glorify God in your body and in your spirit, which are God's. . . . If we live in the Spirit, let us also walk in the Spirit. . . . But we all, with unveiled face, beholding as in a mirror the glory of the Lord, are being transformed into the same image from glory to glory, just as by the Spirit of the Lord. (Romans 8:13–14; 1 Corinthians 6:19–20; Galatians 5:25; 2 Corinthians 4:18)

Words such as these define the operations of the Spirit. As God is first known by His works, so it is with the Spirit. He reveals God's will, Christ doing that will and calling us to follow Him in it. As the believer surrenders himself to a life in the Spirit and willingly consents to the leading of the Spirit, the mortifying of the flesh, the obedience to the rule of Christ without limit or exception, he will become what he gives himself to. As he waits on the Spirit, he will know the Spirit's working in him. It is as we simply make the focus of the Holy Spirit our focus and give ourselves entirely to what He has come to do in us that we are prepared to know His indwelling presence. It will be the Spirit himself bearing witness with our spirit as we are led by Him to obey God even as Christ did.

We shall also know Him more certainly and intimately as we not only yield ourselves to the life He lives in us but also as we study the personal relationship that a believer has with Him and the way in which His ministry in us may most fully be experienced. The habit of soul that the Spirit desires in us is expressed in one word: *faith*. Faith always has to do with the invisible, with what appears to us most unlikely. When the divine appeared in Jesus, it was hidden in a lowly form. For the thirty years He lived in Nazareth they saw nothing in Him but the son of a carpenter. It was only with His baptism that His divine sonship came to the forefront. Even to His disciples His divine glory was often hidden. How much more when the life of God enters the depths of our sinful being will it be a matter of faith to recognize it! And so may we know the Spirit's presence by a humble faith. But let us not be content only to *know* that the Spirit is in us; let us cultivate the habit in our spiritual disciplines of bowing in silence before God, giving the Spirit the recognition that is due Him and not allow the influence of the flesh to overshadow our service to God. Let us wait on the Spirit in holy dependence, and in quiet meditation enter the temple of our heart to see whether all is surrendered to Him. As we bow before the Father, we may ask and expect from Him the ministry of the Holy Spirit. However little we see or feel with our natural senses, let us believe with our whole heart. The divine is first known by faith. As we continue to believe, we will feel and see as well.

There is no way of knowing what a fruit is like until we taste it. We cannot truly know an individual except by close relationship. So we cannot know the things of the Spirit unless we fellowship with Him and He with us. To live in the Spirit is the only way to know the Spirit.

For the full knowledge of Christ Jesus, Paul counted all things but loss. And so must we. We must give all to know the glorified Christ through the Spirit. The Father has sent the Spirit that we might fully share in the glory of Christ. May we all find the will and the desire to yield ourselves fully to the indwelling and teaching of the blessed Spirit whom the Son has given.

Blessed Father, you who have in the name of Christ sent us your Holy Spirit, graciously hear my prayer and grant that I may know Him indeed by His indwelling presence. May His witness to Jesus be divinely clear and may His leading and sanctifying be in such power that the consciousness of Him as my life may be as sure as my natural life. As light is sufficient witness to the sun, may His light be its own witness to the presence of Jesus.

Lead me, O Father, that in knowing Him I may know more fully the mystery of your love. Teach me and all your people to know your Spirit—not only to know that He is in us or to know somewhat of His work, but to know Him as a person, the one who reveals and glorifies the Son. Amen.

Summary

1. A church or a believer may have a correct comprehension of all that Scripture says about the Holy Spirit, may know of Him, and yet not be convinced that He is the divine revelation of a present Christ as Savior and King.
2. The Word alone cannot teach us to know the Spirit. The Word is the test. But to apply the test of the Word, we need with certainty to know the Spirit and that it is He who teaches us.
3. "The natural man does not receive the things of the Spirit of God, for they are foolishness to him; nor can he know them, because they are spiritually discerned" (1 Corinthians 2:14). The spirit of the world and its wisdom cannot know the Spirit of God. A spirit must be born of God to know the Spirit that comes from heaven.
4. Would you know the Spirit? Remember, He will reveal himself if you will submit to the laws of His indwelling. These are simple. Believe that He dwells in you and reaffirm that fact by faith continually. Yield yourself wholeheartedly to His leading, as to one who has sole guidance of your life. Wait then, in dependence upon His further teaching and the fuller experience of His indwelling and work.
5. If we believe He is a person of the Trinity, we must treat Him as such, relate to Him as a person, glorify Him in our hearts as a person, give Him the full expression of our love, and converse with Him as we would a person. Let us especially fear to grieve Him.

Chapter 9

The Spirit of Truth

But when the Helper comes, whom I shall send to you
from the Father, the Spirit of truth who proceeds
from the Father, He will testify of Me.

John 15:26

However, when He, the Spirit of truth, has come, He will
guide you into all truth; for He will not speak on His own
authority, but whatever He hears He will speak;
and He will tell you things to come.

John 16:13

God created man in His image to become like himself, capable of having fellowship with Him. In the garden of Eden two ways were set before man for attaining to this likeness to God. These were typified by the two trees: the tree of life and the tree of the knowledge of good and evil. God's way was the former: Through life would come the knowledge and likeness of God; in abiding in God's will and partaking of God's life, man would be perfected. In recommending the other, Satan assured man that knowledge was the one thing to be desired to make us like God. When man chose the light of knowledge above the life of obedience, he entered upon the terrible path that leads to death. The desire to know became his greatest temptation; his whole nature was corrupted, and knowledge was to him more than obedience and more than life.

Under the power of this deceit, which promises happiness in knowledge, the human race is still led astray. Nowhere does it show its power more terribly than in connection with true religion and God's revelation of himself. Even when the Word of God is accepted, the wisdom of the world and of the flesh still enter in; even spiritual truth is robbed of its power when held, not in the life of the Spirit, but in the wisdom of man.

Where truth enters the inward parts, as God desires it to, it becomes the life of the spirit. But it is possible for it only to reach the outer parts of the soul, the intellect and reason. While it may satisfy the imagination it will be nothing more than one of many ways or means of human argument and wisdom that never reaches to the true life of the spirit. There is a truth of the understanding and feelings that is only natural, the human image or form, the shadow of divine truth. There is a truth that is substance and reality, communicating to him who holds it the actual possession of the *life* of the things that others only think and speak of. The truth in shadow, in form, in thought, was all the law could give; and in that the religion of the Jews consisted. The truth of substance, the truth as a divine life, was what Jesus brought as the only-begotten, full of grace and truth. He is himself the truth.

In promising the Holy Spirit to His disciples, our Lord

speaks of Him as the Spirit of truth. That truth, which He himself is, that truth and grace and life that He brought from heaven as a substantial spiritual reality to communicate to us, has its existence in the Spirit of God: He is the Spirit, the inner life of that divine truth. When we receive Him, and just as fully as we receive Him and give ourselves to Him, He makes Christ and the life of God to be truth in us divinely realized. In His teaching and guiding into the truth, He does not give us only words, thoughts, images, or impressions coming to us from without, from a book or a teacher. He enters the deeper roots of our life and plants the truth of God there as a seed and dwells in it as divine life. When in faith, expectation, and surrender this hidden life is cherished and nourished, He quickens and strengthens it so that it grows stronger and spreads its influence throughout the whole being. Therefore, not from without but from within, not in word but in power, in life and truth, the Spirit reveals Christ and all He has for us. He makes Christ, who to some has been only an image or a thought, a Savior who is outside and above us, to be truth *within* us. The Spirit brings with Him the truth, and then having possessed us from within, guides us, as we can grasp it, into all truth.

In His promise to send the Spirit of truth from the Father, our Lord tells us what the Spirit's principal work will be. It is to bear witness of Him: "Whatever He hears He will speak" (John 16:13). Two chapters earlier He had said, "I am the way, the truth, and the life" (14:6); the Spirit of truth can have no work but to reveal and impart the fullness of grace and truth that are in Christ. He came down from the glorified Lord in heaven to bear witness within us, and so through us, of the reality and power of the redemption that Christ accomplished there. There are Christians who fear that thinking or speaking too much of the Spirit's presence within will lead them away from the Savior. Looking within ourselves may do this, but we may be sure that recognition of the Spirit within us will only lead to a fuller, greater assurance that Christ alone is all in all. It is the Spirit who will make our knowledge of Christ to be life and truth.

The disposition or state of mind in which we fully receive this guidance into all truth is found in the remarkable words of our text concerning the Spirit: "He will guide you into all truth; for He will not speak on His own authority, but whatever He hears He will speak." The mark of the Spirit of truth is divine teachableness. In the mystery of the Holy Trinity there is nothing more beautiful than this: With a divine equality on the part of the Son and the Spirit, there is also a perfect subordination. The Son could claim that men should honor Him even as they honored the Father and yet count it no lessening of that honor to say, "The Son can do nothing of Himself, but what He sees the Father do" (John 5:19). Likewise, the Spirit of truth never speaks from himself. We may think He surely could speak from himself, but He only speaks what He hears. The Spirit that does not speak on His own, that listens for God to speak, and only speaks when God speaks, this is the Spirit of truth.

This is the disposition He effects in those who truly receive Him: a gentle teachableness that marks the humble in spirit who have come to realize that as worthless as their own righteousness is, so is their wisdom or power to grasp spiritual truth. They acknowledge that they need Christ as much for the one as for the other and that the Spirit within them alone is the Spirit of truth. He shows us how, even with the Word of God in our hands and on our tongues, we may be lacking in that submissive spirit to which alone the Word's spiritual meaning is revealed. He opens our eyes to the reason why so much Bible reading, knowledge, and preaching has so little fruit unto true holiness: It is accomplished apart from the wisdom that is from above. The mark of the Spirit of truth is lacking. The Spirit receives all that it speaks and teaches day by day, step by step, from God the Father.

These thoughts suggest to us a great danger of the Christian life—seeking to know the truth of God in His Word without waiting on the Spirit of truth. The tempter of the garden still moves among us. Knowledge is still his prime temptation to God's people. How many Christians would confess that their knowledge of divine truth does little for them, leaving them powerless against sin and the world? They have not experienced the light and freedom, the strength and joy the truth was meant to bring. It is because they seek to know God's truth through the power of human wisdom instead of waiting on the Spirit of truth to lead them. Most earnest efforts to abide in Christ, to walk like Christ, fail when we depend more on the wisdom of this world than on the power of God.

These thoughts suggest a great need in the Christian life. Jesus said, "If anyone desires to come after Me, let him deny himself . . . and follow Me" (Matthew 16:24). Many seek to follow Jesus without denying themselves. There is nothing that needs our denial more than our own wisdom, the energy of a worldly mind, as it exerts itself in the things of God.

May we learn that in all our fellowship with God, in His Word or in prayer, in every act of worship, our first step ought to be a solemn act of self-denial, in which we give up our power to understand God's Word, or even to speak our words to Him, without the divine leading of the Holy Spirit. This is the meaning of the call to be silent before God and quietly wait on Him, to quiet the rush of thoughts and words in God's presence, in deep humility and stillness to wait, listen, and hear what God will say.

O Lord of truth, who seeks truth in the inward parts of those who worship Him, I thank you again that you have given me the Spirit of truth and that He dwells in me. I ask that I may know Him fully and walk before you in the living consciousness that the Spirit of truth, the Spirit of Christ, who is the truth, is indeed within me, the inmost self of my new life. May every thought and word, every disposition and habit, be testimony that the Spirit of Christ dwells and rules within me.

May the truth of your atonement as it works with living efficacy in the upper sanctuary, dwell in me and I in it. May your life and glory no less be truth in me, a living experience of your presence and power.

I bow before you, asking that according to the riches of your glory you may work mightily in me and in all your saints. That all may know their privilege and rejoice in it: the Holy Spirit within them to reveal Christ, full of grace and truth. Amen.

Summary

1. Just as physical sight is a function of a healthy natural life, so spiritual light comes only in a healthy spiritual life. Life truths can only be known by living them; the Spirit of life, only by living in the Spirit. Where faith exercises itself in accepting and yielding to the life of the Spirit in the hidden part, the new spirit, there its ear will be opened and the voice of the Spirit will be heard. The Spirit of life is the Spirit of truth, *within you,* in your innermost being.

2. Sin has a twofold effect: It is not only guilt, but death; it 7not only works legal condemnation from above, but moral corruption within. Redemption is not only righteousness but life: not only objective but subjective restoration to God's favor and fellowship. The first is the work of the Son for us, the second of the Spirit of the Son within us. There are many who cling firmly to the work of the Son and yet fail to receive the peace and the power He gives because they do not fully yield to the work of the Spirit in them. As full and clear as our acceptance of the divine atoning Savior must be our assurance of the divine indwelling Spirit to make our Savior's work truth in us. The Spirit of truth within us is the Spirit of Christ.

3. We know God desires truth in the inward parts (our inmost being), and there He will make us to know wisdom. Truth and wisdom are not to be mere understanding, but in the inward hidden life of the Spirit. The Spirit of truth, dwelling in us, is the fulfillment of this prophecy.

Chapter 10

The Expediency of the Spirit's Coming

Nevertheless I tell you the truth. It is to your advantage
that I go away; for if I do not go away, the Helper will not
come to you; but if I depart, I will send Him to you.

John 16:7

When our Lord left this world, He promised the disciples that His departure would be their gain; the Helper [called the Comforter in some versions] would take His place and be to them far better than He ever had been or could be by His physical presence. This would be true particularly in two aspects. His fellowship with them had never been unbroken, but liable to interruption; now it would be broken off by death and they would not see Him again. But the Spirit would abide with them forever. His own communion with them had been very external, and because of this had not resulted in what might have been expected. The Spirit would be in them; His coming would be as an indwelling presence, in the power of which they would have

Jesus with them, too, as their life and strength.

During the life of our Lord on earth, each of His disciples was ministered to by Him in accordance with his individual character and the special circumstances in which he might be placed. The fellowship with each one was intensely personal. In everything He proved that He knew His sheep by name. For each there was shown thoughtfulness and wisdom that supplied what was needed. Would the Spirit also supply these needs with the same personal interest and special individual attention that made Jesus' guidance so precious? There was no doubt. All that Christ was to them the Spirit would be in even greater power and blessedness that would never cease. They would be happier, safer, even stronger than when Jesus walked with them on earth. The indwelling of the Spirit was meant to restore Christ's most personal communion and guidance, even His personal friendship.

It is to many a matter of great difficulty to conceive of this fact, much less believe it and experience it. The thought of Christ walking with men and women on earth, fellowshipping with them and guiding them, is clear. The thought of the Spirit indwelling us and speaking in the secret depths of our being makes His guidance more difficult to grasp.

And yet what constitutes the difficulty of the new spiritual communion and guidance is what gives it its greater worth and blessedness. It is the same principle found in daily life: Difficulty calls upon dormant powers, strengthens the will, develops character, and makes the person. In a child's first lessons he is helped and encouraged; as the lessons increase in difficulty, the teacher may leave him to exercise his own skills and to call upon his own resources.

A young person eventually leaves his parents' home to test the principles that have been instilled in him since childhood. In each case it is expedient that the outward presence and help be withdrawn and the individual be thrown upon himself to apply and assimilate the lessons he has been taught.

God indeed wants to educate us to a perfect manhood—not ruled by an outward law but by the inner life. As long as Jesus was with the disciples on earth, He had to work with them from without, never effectually reaching the innermost being. When He went away, He sent the Spirit to be in them so that their growth might be from within. Taking possession first of the innermost recesses of their being by His Spirit, He would have them in the voluntary consent and surrender to His inspiration and guidance. So they would have the framing of their life—the forming of their character—in their own hands, in the power of the divine Spirit, who really had become their spirit. They would grow up to true self-confidence—independence from outward influences—in which they would become like Christ, who having life in himself lived in full dependence on the Father.

As long as the Christian asks only for what is easy and pleasant, he will never understand that it is better for us that Christ is not with us on the earth. But as soon as the thoughts of difficulty and sacrifice are set aside in the honest desire to become a truly godlike person, bearing the full image of the Son and living well-pleasing to the Father, the thought of Jesus' departure that His Spirit may become our own will be welcomed with gladness and gratitude. If to follow the leading of the Spirit, and particularly the personal friendship and guidance of Jesus, is a more difficult path than it would have been to follow Him on earth, we must remember the privilege we enjoy, the nobility we attain, the intimacy of fellowship with God we enter into as infinitely greater. To have the Holy Spirit of God coming through the human nature of our Lord, entering into our spirits, identifying himself with us and becoming our own just as He was the Spirit of Christ on earth—surely this is a blessing worth any sacrifice, for it is the beginning of the indwelling of God himself.

To see that it is such a privilege and to desire it very earnestly does not remove the difficulty. So the question comes up again: The fellowship of Jesus with His disciples on earth—so condescending in its tenderness, so particular in its interest, so personal in its love—how can this be ours to the same degree now that He is absent and the Spirit is our guide? The answer is simply this: by faith. With Jesus on earth, the disciples, once they had believed, walked by sight. We walk by faith. In faith we must accept and rejoice in the word of Jesus: "It is to your advantage that I go away." We must take time to let it become part of us, to rejoice that He is gone to the Father. Let us thank and praise Him that He has called us to this life in the Spirit. Believe that in this gift of the Spirit the presence and fellowship of our Lord are provided for us most effectually. It may indeed be in a way we do not yet understand because we have so cautiously believed and rejoiced in the gift of the Holy Spirit. But faith must believe and praise for what it does not yet understand. Be confident and joyful that the Holy Spirit, and Jesus himself through Him, will teach us how the fellowship and guidance are to be experienced.

We must be careful not to misunderstand the word that the Spirit will teach us. We generally connect teaching with thoughts. We want the Spirit to suggest to us certain concepts of how Jesus will be with us and in us. This is not what He does. The Spirit does not dwell in the mind but in the life; not in what we know but in what we are. Do not seek or expect at once a clear apprehension, a new insight, into this or any divine truth. Knowledge, thought, feeling, action—all are a part of that external walk the presence of Jesus wrought in the disciples. The Spirit came, and deeper than all of these, He was to be the hidden presence of Jesus within the depths of their personalities. The divine life in newness of power was to become the life of the disciples. The teaching of the Spirit would begin not in word or thought, but in power. It would be the power of a life working in them in secret but with divine energy, the power of a faith that rejoices that Jesus is near and taking charge of one's whole life and every circumstance. The Spirit would inspire them with the faith of the indwelling Jesus. This would be the beginning of His teaching. They would have the life of Jesus within them and they would know by faith that it was Jesus. Their faith would be both the cause and effect of the presence of the Lord by the Spirit.

It is by such a faith—a faith born of the Spirit—that the presence of Jesus is made as real and all-sufficient as when He was on earth. Why is it that believers who have the Spirit do not experience His presence more consciously and fully? The answer is simple: they scarcely know and honor the Spirit who is in them. They have faith in Jesus who died, who reigns in heaven, but little faith in Jesus who dwells in them by His Spirit. We need more faith in Jesus as the fulfiller of the promise "He who believes in Me, as the Scripture has said, out of his heart will flow rivers of living water" (John 7:38). We must believe that the Holy Spirit is within us as the presence of our Lord Jesus. And we must not only believe this with the faith of our understanding—as it seeks to persuade itself of the truth of what Christ says—but we must believe with the heart, a heart in which the Holy Spirit dwells. The whole gift of the Spirit, the whole teaching of Jesus concerning the Spirit is to enforce the message "The kingdom of God is within you" (Luke 17:21). If we would have true faith of the heart, we must look within and humbly yield to the Holy Spirit to do His work in us.

To receive this teaching and this faith that stands in the life and power of the Spirit, we will above all fear what hinders Him most: the will and the wisdom of men. We are surrounded by a life of self—of the flesh—in the service of God. Even in our efforts to exercise faith, the flesh puts itself forward, flaunting its own strength. Every thought, whether good or evil, in which our mind runs before the Spirit, must be brought into captivity. Lay your own will and your own wisdom captive at the feet of Jesus and wait in faith and stillness of soul. The deep consciousness will grow that the Spirit is within you and that His divine life is living and growing in you. As we honor Him and give ourselves to Him, as we bring our activities in the flesh into subjection to Him, He will not put us to shame, but do His work in us. He will strengthen our inner life, quicken our faith, reveal Jesus, and we shall, step by step, learn that the presence and personal communion and guidance of Jesus are ours as clear and as precious—even more so—as they were when He was here on earth.

Lord Jesus, though I did not know you on the earth as the disciples did, I acknowledge that fellowship with you is more real, more near, more tender, more effectual than if you were still here on earth. I praise you that your Holy Spirit dwells within me and allows me to know what that fellowship is— the reality of your perfect indwelling.

Holy Lord! Forgive me that I have not praised and loved you fully for this most wonderful gift and the Father's love. Teach me with an expectant faith to believe in you from whom, day by day, the fresh anointing flows and fills my life.

Hear me, Lord, when I cry to you on behalf of so many of your redeemed who do not yet see what it is to give up their life after the flesh, to receive in its place the life that is in the power of the Spirit. With many others I ask that you awaken the church to know the mark of her election, the secret of her enjoyment of your presence, the power for fulfilling her calling: that each believer might be led to know the Spirit who dwells within. The abiding presence of the Lord with us as keeper, guide, and friend is indeed our sure reward. Grant it, Lord, for your name's sake. Amen.

Summary

1. The fact that the Helper would not come if Jesus did not go away is convincing proof that the gift of the Spirit on the day of Pentecost is something distinct from anything before that time—a new dispensation.
2. The knowledge the disciples had of Jesus on earth was something so blessed and divine that they could not

conceive of there being anything better. They could only think with sorrow of the prospect of losing what they knew to be of God. There are many evangelical Christians who must also give up the knowledge they have previously had of Christ if He is to be revealed to them in the power of the Holy Spirit. "Because I have said these things to you, sorrow has filled your heart. Nevertheless I tell you the truth. It is to your advantage that I go away; for if I do not go away, the Helper will not come to you; but if I depart, I will send Him to you" (John 16:6–7). These words can only be fully understood when they have become a personal experience. A mere external knowledge of Christ by which we have known a life of effort and failure must make way for the spiritual indwelling.

3. The law of the kingdom is through death to life, losing all to gain the more. The great hindrance to many Christians is their trust in the orthodoxy and sufficiency of their religious knowledge. If they, as they say, could only be more earnest and faithful. . . . But notice that in the life of the disciples, new and more strenuous efforts would only have led to new and more bitter failures. They, though true disciples, had to let go, to die to their old way of knowing Christ, and to receive as a gift an entirely new life of fellowship with Him. If Christians today could only see the more excellent way of living a holy life: through the indwelling Spirit of Christ, revealing and maintaining in them the presence of their Lord in power.

Chapter 11

The Spirit
Glorifies Christ

*He will glorify Me, for He will take of what is Mine
and declare it to you.*

John 16:14

The Scripture speaks of a twofold glorifying of the Son. The one is by the Father, the other by the Spirit: the one takes place in heaven, the other here on earth. By the one He is glorified "in God himself"; by the other, "in us" (John 13:32; 17:10). Of the former Jesus said: "If God is glorified in Him [the Son of Man], God will also glorify Him in Himself, and glorify Him immediately." And again, in the high-priestly prayer, "Father, the hour has come. Glorify Your Son. . . . And now, O Father, glorify me together with Yourself" (John 17:1, 5). Of the latter He said, "He will glorify Me, for He will take of what is Mine and declare it to you."

To glorify is to manifest the hidden excellence and worth of a person. Jesus, the Son of Man, was to be glorified when

His human nature was admitted to the full participation of the power and glory in which God dwells. He entered into the perfect spirit-life of the heavenly world, of the divine being. All the angels worshiped Him as the Lamb on the throne. Of this heavenly, spiritual glory of Christ, the human mind cannot conceive or apprehend. It can only be truly known by experience, by being communicated to and appropriated in the inner life. This is the work of the Holy Spirit, as the Spirit of the glorified Christ. He comes to us as the Spirit of glory and reveals the glory of Christ in us by dwelling and working in us. He makes Christ glorious to us and in us. Likewise, He glorifies Him in us and through us in those who have eyes to see. The Son seeks not His own glory: The Father glorifies Him in heaven, the Spirit glorifies Him in our hearts.

But before the Spirit could glorify Christ, He first needed to go away from His disciples. They could not have Him in the flesh and in the Spirit, too; His physical presence would hinder the spiritual indwelling. They had to part with the Christ they knew and loved before they could receive the indwelling Christ glorified by the Holy Spirit. Christ himself had to give up the life He had before He could be glorified in heaven or in us. Even in union with Him, we must give up the measure of the life we have had in Him if we are to have Him glorified to us and in us by the Holy Spirit.

I am persuaded that at this point many of God's children need the teaching: "It is to your advantage that I go away." Like His disciples, they have believed in Jesus; they love and obey Him; they have experienced much of the inexpressible blessedness of knowing and following Him.

And yet they feel that the deep rest and joy, the holy light and the divine power of His abiding indwelling, as they see it in Holy Scripture, is not yet theirs. First in secret and then under the blessed influence of the fellowship of the saints, the teaching of God's servants has been helped and wonderfully blessed. Christ has become very precious. And yet they see something still before them—promises not yet fulfilled, wants not fully satisfied. The reason for this could be that they have not yet fully inherited the promise "When He, the Spirit of truth, has come, He will guide you into all truth; for He will not speak on His own authority, but whatever He hears He will speak; and He will tell you things to come. He will glorify Me, for He will take of what is Mine and declare it to you" (John 16:13–14). They do not fully understand the expediency of Christ's going away to come again glorified in the Spirit. They have not yet been able to say that though they have known Christ after the flesh, yet now they do not know Him.

Knowing Christ after the flesh must come to an end. We must make way for knowing Him in the power of the Spirit. "After the flesh" means in the power of the external, relating to words and thoughts, efforts and feelings, influences and helps coming from without. The believer who has received the Holy Spirit but does not know fully what this implies and so does not give himself entirely to His leading, to a great extent has confidence only in the flesh. Admitting that he can do nothing without the Spirit, he still labors and struggles vainly to believe and live as he knows he should. Confessing his sins sincerely, and at times experiencing in a most blessed way that Christ alone is his life and strength, it grieves him to think how often he fails in the maintenance of that attitude of trustful dependence by which Christ can live out His life in him. He seeks to believe all that he knows of Christ's presence and keeping and indwelling, and yet somehow there are still breaks and interruptions; it is as if faith is not what it should be—the substance of things hoped for. The reason must be that faith itself is still too much the work of the mind, in the power of the flesh, in the wisdom of men. There has been a revelation of Christ the faithful keeper, the abiding friend, but that revelation has been, in part, appropriated by the flesh and the natural mind. This has made the revelation powerless. The Christ of glory, the doctrine of the indwelling Christ, has been received only partly by the spirit. Only the Spirit of Christ can glorify Christ. We must give up the old way of knowing Christ. We must know Him no more after the flesh.

What does it mean that the Spirit glorifies Christ? We read in Hebrews:

> But we see Jesus, who was made a little lower than the angels, for the suffering of death *crowned with glory and honor,* that He, by the grace of God, might taste death for everyone. For it was fitting for Him, for whom are all things and by whom are all things, in bringing many sons to glory, to make the captain of their salvation perfect through sufferings. (Hebrews 2:9–10, emphasis added)

To Him all things have been made subject. So our Lord connects His being glorified, in the passage we have taken as our text, with all things being given to Him. "He will glorify Me, for He will take of what is Mine and declare it to you. All things that the Father has are Mine. Therefore I said that He will take of Mine and declare it to you" (John 16:14–15). In exalting Him above all rule and power and dominion, the Father has put all things in subjection under His feet: He gave unto Him the name that is above every name, that at the name of Jesus every knee should bow. The kingdom and the power and the glory are one: Unto Him that sits on the throne, and to the Lamb in the midst of the throne, are the glory and the dominion forever. It is as sitting on the throne of the divine glory, with all things put in subjection under His feet, that Jesus has been glorified in heaven. (See Ephesians 1:20–22; Philippians 2:9–10.)

When the Holy Spirit glorifies Jesus in us, He reveals Him to us in His glory. He takes of the things of Christ and declares them to us. It is not that He gives us a thought, image, or vision of that glory as it is in heaven, but He shows it to us as a personal experience and possession. He enables us to partake of it in our innermost being. He shows Christ as present in us. All the true, living knowledge we have of Christ is through the Spirit of God. After our first knowledge of Christ, and after we have invited Him into our heart, He grows and increases and is formed within us; when we learn to trust and follow and serve Him—this, too, is all of the Holy Spirit. All of this, however, may exist, even as it did in the disciples, with a certain amount of darkness and failure. But when the Holy Spirit does His perfect work and reveals the glorified Lord, the throne of His glory is set up in the heart and He rules over every enemy. Every power is brought into subjection, every thought into captivity to the obedience of Christ. Through the whole of the renewed nature there rises the song,

"Glory to Him who sits on the throne." Though the confession holds true to the end, "In me, that is, in my flesh, dwells no good thing," the holy presence of Christ as ruler and governor so fills the heart and life that His authority rules over all. Sin has no power. The law of the Spirit of life in Christ Jesus has made me free from the law of sin and death.

If this is the glorifying of Christ that the Spirit brings, it is easy to see the way that leads to it. The enthronement of Jesus in His glory can take place only in the heart that has promised implicit and unreserved obedience. It is in the heart that has had the courage to believe that He will reign, and in faith that expects every enemy to be kept under His feet. It claims and accepts Christ as Lord of all, everything in life, great or small, taken possession of and guided by Him, through His Holy Spirit. It is in the loving, obedient disciple the Spirit promises to dwell; in him the Spirit glorifies Christ.

This takes place in God's perfect timing in the believing soul. The history of the church as a whole repeats itself in each individual. Until the time appointed of the Father, who has the times and seasons in His own hands, the heir is under guardians and stewards, and does not differ from a bondservant. When the fullness of time is come and faith is perfected, the Spirit of the glorified One enters in power and Christ dwells in the heart. Yes, the history of Christ himself repeats itself in the soul. In the temple there were two holy places—the one before the veil, the other within the veil, the Holy of Holies. In His earthly life Christ dwelt and ministered in the Holy Place outside the veil: the veil of the flesh kept Him out of the Most Holy. It was only when the veil of the flesh was rent that He could enter the inner sanctuary of the full glory of the Spirit-life in heaven.

Likewise, the believer who longs to have Jesus glorified within by the Spirit must, however blessed his life has been in the knowledge and service of his Lord, learn that there is something better. In him, too, the veil of the flesh must be rent; he must enter into this work of Christ through the new and living way into the Holiest of All. The soul must see how completely Jesus has triumphed over the flesh and entered into the Spirit-life. It must realize how perfect, in virtue of that triumph, His power is over all in our flesh that might hinder, and how perfect in the power of the Spirit the entrance and the indwelling of Jesus can be. The veil is taken away and the life before lived in the Holy Place is now one in the Most Holy, in the full presence of His glory.

This rending of the veil, this enthronement of Jesus as the glorified one in the heart, is not always with trumpet sound and shout. It may be so at times, and with some individuals, but in others it takes place with deep awe and stillness, where not a sound is heard. Zion's king still comes meek and lowly, with the kingdom, to the poor in spirit. Without form or comeliness He enters in, and when thought and feeling fail, the Holy Spirit glorifies Him to the faith that sees not but believes. The eye of flesh did not see Him on the throne; to the world it was a mystery; so just when all within appears hopeless and empty, the Spirit secretly works the divine assurance, and then the blessed experience that Christ, the glorified One, has taken up His residence within. The soul knows in silent worship and adoration that Jesus is Master, that His throne in the heart is established in righteousness and the promise is now fulfilled.

Blessed Lord Jesus, I worship you in the glory that the Father has given you. I bless you for the promise that your glory shall be revealed in the hearts of your people to dwell in them and fill them. This is your glory, that all that the Father has is now yours in its infinite fullness and power. You have said that the Holy Spirit will take it and show it unto us. Heaven and earth are full of your glory. The hearts and lives of your beloved may be filled with it, too. Lord, let it be so!

Blessed be your holy name for all in whom the rich beginnings of the fulfillment have already come! Lord, let it go on from glory to glory.

To this end, teach us, we pray, to maintain our separation unto you unbroken: Heart and life shall be yours alone. To this end teach us to hold fast our confidence without wavering, that the Spirit who is within us will perfect His work. Above all, teach us to yield ourselves in ever-increasing dependency on the Spirit's teaching and leading. We desire to have no confidence in the flesh, its wisdom or its righteousness. We bow before you in holy fear and reverence of the truth that your Holy Spirit is within us to do His divine work. Let Him rise in great power and have authority within us so that our heart may be the temple in which you alone are glorified. Amen.

Summary

1. It was the true Christ these disciples knew, and to a certain degree it was a true knowledge of Christ they had (see Matthew 16). It was a knowledge that influenced them strongly, drawing them to follow Him and love

Him. But it was not full knowledge; that is, the knowledge in Spirit and in truth; nor yet the spiritual knowledge of Christ glorified and abiding in them through the Holy Spirit. This constitutes the second blessing.

2. Oh, that God would teach us this lesson: The one great work of the Spirit, as the Spirit of Christ, is to make the glorified Christ always present in us—not in our thoughts or memory only, but within us, in our innermost being, in our life and experience.

3. Can it be? Jesus, the glorified One, always present with us, dwelling *in* us? Yes, it can be. The Holy Spirit has been given by the Father for this work. And He dwells in us. Let us believe, let us bask in that wonderful indwelling.

4. Let us bow in submission to His leading, waiting for His teaching, reverently honoring His holy presence within us, even when we cannot see or feel it.

Chapter 12

The Spirit
Convicts of Sin

And when [the Helper, the Comforter] has come,
He will convict the world of sin, and of
righteousness, and of judgment.

John 16:8

The close connection between this passage and the one that precedes it is not always noticed. Before the Holy Spirit was to convict the world of sin, He was to come to the disciples. Jesus would be returned to His Father, and the Holy Spirit would be sent to take His place in their lives. He was to make His home in them, and through them begin His work of conviction in the world. The disciples would come to realize that the work of the Holy Spirit—striving with men and convicting the world of sin—could only be done as He had a firm footing on earth *in them*. They were to be baptized with the Holy Spirit and with fire; would receive the power from on high with the sole purpose of making them instruments through whom the Holy Spirit could reach the world. The sin-convicting power of the Spirit was to dwell in them and work through them. It was for this our Lord sought to prepare them and us by these words.

First of all, as we have said, the Holy Spirit comes to us, that through us He may reach others. The Spirit is the Spirit of the Holy One, the redeeming God. When He makes His home in us, He does not change His nature or lose His divine character. He is still the Spirit of God striving with men and seeking their deliverance. Wherever He is not hindered by ignorance or selfishness, He radiates from our hearts, His temple, for the work He will do in the world. He makes us willing and bold to do His work; to testify against sin and *for* Jesus, the Savior from sin. He does this as the Spirit of the crucified and exalted Christ. Isaiah said, "The Spirit of the Lord is upon Me, Because He has anointed Me to preach the gospel to the poor; He has sent Me to heal the brokenhearted, to proclaim liberty to the captives and recovery of sight to the blind, to set at liberty those who are oppressed; to proclaim the acceptable year of the Lord" (Luke 4:18–19, from Isaiah 61:1–2). It was this same Spirit—through whom Christ had offered himself unto God, and through whom He had been raised from the dead. The Spirit would have a home in the disciples as He had in Christ. And in no lesser way than in Christ would the divine Spirit in them pursue His divine work. As a light shining in the darkness, revealing, condemning, and conquering—and as "the Spirit of burning and the Spirit of judgment," He is to the world the power of divine conviction and conversion. Not so much directly from heaven as the Spirit of God, but as the Holy Spirit dwelling in the church.

Second, the Spirit can reach others only through us by first bringing us into perfect harmony with himself. He enters into us to become so *one* with us that He becomes as a disposition or life within us. Then His work in us and through us to others becomes identical with our work.

The application of this truth to the conviction of sin in the world is one of great importance. The words of our Lord are frequently applied to believers in reference to the continued conviction of sin that He would work within them. In this sense they are most applicable. This work of the Spirit remains throughout the undertone of all His comforting and sanctifying work. It is only as He keeps alive sensitivity to the danger and shame of sin that the soul will be kept in a place of humility before God—hiding in Jesus, as it were, as its only safety and strength. As the Holy Spirit reveals and communicates the holy life of Christ within, the result will be a deeper sense of the gravity of sin. But the words mean more. If the Spirit through us, through our testimony, whether by word or walk, is to convict the world, He must first convince us of the world's sin. He must first give us a sight and sense of the guilt of the world's unbelief and rejection of the Savior. We must see and sense its sins as the cause, the proof, and the fruit of that rejection so that we will in some measure think and feel in regard to sin as He does. There will then be an inner preparedness for the Spirit to work through us; a unity between our witness and His witness *against* sin and *for* God, which alone will convince the conscience and convict with a power that is from above.

We know how easy it is, in the power of the flesh, to judge others—to see the speck in the eye of another while we miss the beam in our own. And if we are indeed free from what we condemn in others, we say by our actions, "I am higher and holier than you." We either testify and work in a wrong spirit and in our own strength, or we don't have the courage to work at all. It is because we see the sin and the sinfulness of others without the conviction that comes from the Holy Spirit. When He convinces us of the sin of the world, His work bears two marks. The first is a sacrifice of self, in jealousy for God and His honor, combined with a deep and real grief for the guilty. The second is a firm, strong faith in the possibility and power of deliverance. We see sin in its terrible relation to the whole; we see the whole in the double light of the cross. We see sin unspeakably hateful in its affront against God and its power over the weakened soul, and we see sin condemned, atoned for, put away, and conquered in Jesus. We learn to look on the world as God looks upon it in His holiness. We hate sin with an infinite hatred, but we love the sinner with the love that sent His Son. The Son gives life, destroys sin, and sets its captive free.

May God give His people a true and deep conviction of the sin of the world in its rejection of Christ as fitting preparation for the Spirit's using them in convicting the world of sin.

Third, to obtain this conviction of sin, the believer must not only pray for it but also have his whole life under the leading of the Holy Spirit. We cannot too earnestly declare that the various gifts of the Spirit depend upon His personal indwelling and supremacy in the inner life, and the revelation in us of Christ, who gave His life to see sin destroyed. When our Lord spoke that word of inexhaustible meaning, "He will be in you," He opened up the secret of the Spirit's power to teach, sanctify, and strengthen. The Holy Spirit is the life of God. He enters in and becomes our life. It is desirable and necessary to direct the attention of the believer to the various operations of the Spirit so that he will not neglect or lose anything through lack of knowledge. As well, with each new insight into what the Spirit can do, we need to get a firmer grasp of the truth. Let your life be in the Spirit and His special blessing will not be withheld. If you would like to have this deep spiritual conviction of the sin of the world, the sense of its terrible reality and power and exceeding sinfulness such as will fit you for being one through whom the Spirit can convict sinners, yield your life completely to the authority of the Holy Spirit. Let the thought of the wondrous mystery of the indwelling God quiet your mind and heart into humble fear and worship. Surrender the great enemy that opposes Him—the flesh, the self-life—day by day to Him. Be content to aim at nothing less than being filled with the Spirit of the One who gave himself to death to take away sin; having our whole being and action under His control and inspiration. As your life in the Spirit becomes healthy and strong, and your spiritual insight invigorated, you will see more clearly and feel more keenly what sin is. Your thoughts and feelings will be those of the Holy Spirit: revulsion of sin, deep faith in the redemption of Christ, and deep love of the souls who are lost. You will become ready to give your life to free them. And He will make you a fit instrument for the Spirit's work of convicting the world of sin.

There is one more lesson. We are seeking in this book

to show the way by which all can be filled with the Spirit. Here is one condition: He must dwell in us as One who convicts of sin. Offer yourself to Him to comprehend, feel, and bear the sins of those around you. Allow the sins of the world to be as much your concern as your own sin. Do not their sins dishonor God? Are they not equally provided for in Christ's redemption? And does not the Spirit dwelling in you long to convict them? Just as the Holy Spirit dwelt in the body and nature of Jesus and was the source of what He felt, said, and did, so the Spirit now dwells in believers. The one purpose for which Christ came into the world, and for which the Holy Spirit strives, is that sin may be conquered and its power brought to nothing. This is the purpose for which the baptism of the Spirit and of fire was given—that in and through believers He might convict the world of sin and deliver from it. Put yourself into contact with those who struggle with sin. Meet them in the love and faith of Jesus Christ as a servant and helper to the needy and despondent. Give yourself to show the reality of faith in Christ, the power of His redemption, and the work of the Spirit in the world. Seek the full experience of the indwelling Spirit for the purpose of the Father's work through you. Live in unity with other believers to work and pray that others will be saved from sin. It is this unity and love for one another that will prove to the world that Christ is real.

The comfort and success with which a man lives and carries on his business depends much upon his having suitable housing for it. When the Holy Spirit in a believer finds the whole heart free and given over to Him as a temple, He can through such a life do His great work. Be assured that there is no more certain way to receive a full measure of the Spirit than to be wholly yielded to Him, to let the mind of Christ be in us. What the Spirit was in Him, He seeks to be in us. What was true of Him must in the same measure be true of us.

Christian, would you be filled with the Holy Spirit and seek to have a clear understanding of the Holy Spirit in you, convincing the world of sin? If you identify thoroughly with Him in this, if He sees that He can use you for His glory, if you make His work your work, you may be certain He will dwell in you richly and work in you mightily. The one purpose for which Christ came was to put away sin; the one work for which the Holy Spirit comes to men is to persuade them to give up sin. The believer lives to join the battle against sin, to seek the will of God. Let us be one with Christ and His Spirit in their testimony against sin. A demonstration of the life and Spirit of Christ will have its effect: The holiness and joy, the love and obedience to Christ will convince the world of sin and unbelief. Just as Christ's death, His sacrifice for sin, was the gateway to His glory in the power of the Spirit, so our experience of the Spirit's indwelling will become the gateway to a full life of power and blessing in convicting the world of sin.

Lord Jesus, it is by the presence and power of the Holy Spirit in your people that the world is convicted and convinced of its sin of rejecting you and that sinners are to be brought out of the world to accept you. It is in men and women full of the Holy Spirit, testifying in the power of a holy joy to what you have done for them, that the proof is given that you are indeed at the right hand of God. It is in a body of living witnesses to what you have done for them that the world is to find the irresistible conviction of its sin and guilt. How little the world has seen of this.

We call upon you, in deep humility, Lord Jesus. Awaken your church to the knowledge of its calling so that every believer might prove to the world what power and blessing there is in faith in you.

Lay the burden of the sin of the world heavily upon the hearts of your people that they might live for the opportunity to prove your presence in the world. Take away all that hinders you from manifesting your saving power through us. Your Spirit is come to convince and convict the world of sin. Help us to join Him in this work. Amen.

Summary

1. The great sin of the world is unbelief—rejection of Christ. This is the spirit of the world.

2. Christ has left the world and gone to the Father. But He has left His people full of His Spirit and the power of a holy life. Their confession of Him to whom they owe their life works to convict the world of sin. What fullness of surrender to the Holy Spirit is needed.

3. What is promised is such an outpouring of the Spirit of God as shall not only reveal itself in the consciousness of the disciples but also substantiate itself as an undeniable and wonderful fact to the onlooking world. Is not the greatest thing needed that the Spirit of God should be so poured out on Christ's people that others should be made aware of His presence?

4. To convince the world of the truth of Christianity, it must first be convinced of its sin. It is sin that renders

Christ intelligible. And for this there is not so much needed evidences and arguments but the manifest presence of the Holy Spirit. For this there is needed continued, united, believing prayer that the Father would strengthen us all with might by His Spirit to be His messengers in the world.

Chapter 13

Waiting for the Spirit

And being assembled together with them, He commanded
them not to depart from Jerusalem, but to wait for the
Promise of the Father, "which," He said,
"you have heard from Me."

Acts 1:4

In the life of the Old Testament saints, *waiting* was one of
the common words by which they expressed the attitude of
their souls toward God. They waited *for* God and *upon*
God. Sometimes we find this in Scripture as the language
of an experience: "Truly my soul waits upon God"; "I wait
for the Lord, my soul waits." At other times it is a plea in
prayer: "Lead me; on you do I wait all day. Be gracious unto
us; we have waited for you." Frequently it is an injunction,
encouraging perseverance in a work that is not without difficulty: "Wait on the Lord; wait, I say, on the Lord. Rest in
the Lord, and wait patiently for him." And then again there
is the testimony to the blessedness of the exercise itself:
"Blessed are they who wait upon him. They that wait upon
the Lord will renew their strength."

In His use of the word *wait,* our Lord relates particularly the teaching and experience of the saints who have gone before us with the promise of the Father, the Holy Spirit. What had been so deeply woven into the very substance of the religious life and language of God's people was now to receive a new and higher application. As they waited for the manifestation of God, either in the light of His countenance on their own souls or in special intervention for their deliverance, or in His coming to fulfill His promises to His people, so we too must wait. But now that the Father has been revealed in the Son, and the Son has perfected His redemption, waiting is particularly to be occupied with the fulfillment of the great promise by which the love of the Father and the grace of the Son are revealed and made one—the gift of the indwelling, or the fullness, of the Holy Spirit. We wait on the Father and the Son for an ever-increasing inflowing and working of the blessed Spirit. We wait for the Spirit himself: His moving, leading, and strengthening to reveal the Father and the Son within us and to work through us the holiness and service to which the Father and the Son call us.

He charged them *to wait* for the promise of the Father, which they had heard from Him. It may be asked whether these words have not exclusive reference to the outpouring of the Spirit on the day of Pentecost and whether now that the Spirit has been given to the church, the charge still holds. It could also be argued that for the believer who knows that the Holy Spirit is within him, waiting for the "promise of the Father" is hardly consistent with a conviction that the Spirit has been received and is already resident.

The question and the argument open the way to a lesson of deepest importance. The Holy Spirit is not given to us as a possession of which we have control and can use at our discretion. The Holy Spirit is given to us as *our* Master, who has control of *us*. We do not use Him, He uses us. When we ask for His working, it must be as real and determined as if we were asking for the first time. When God gives His Spirit, He gives himself. When Jesus gave to those who believe in Him the promise of an ever-flowing fountain, He spoke not of a single act of faith that was once for all to make them the independent possessors of the blessing, but He spoke of a life of faith that holds His gifts in living union with himself. And so the word *wait*, with all its varied meaning from the experience of the past, is woven into the very fiber of the new Spirit dispensation. All that the disciples did and felt during those ten days of waiting, and all that they received as its fruit and reward, becomes to us the path and pledge of the life of the Spirit in which we can live. The fullness of the Spirit and our waiting for it are inseparably and forever linked together.

Do we not have an answer to the question of why so many believers know so little of the joy and power of the Holy Spirit? They have not known to wait for it. They have not studied the Master's parting words: He charged them to wait for the promise of the Father. They have longed for its fulfillment. In earnest prayer they have pleaded for it. They have been burdened and grieved under the felt need. They have tried to believe, tried to lay hold, and tried to be filled with the Spirit. But they have never known what it was to wait. They have never said, or heard, "Blessed are all they that wait for Him. They that wait on the Lord shall renew their strength."

But what is this waiting? And how are we to wait? I look to God by His Holy Spirit to enable me to share in the simplest way possible what may help some child of His to obey this command. Let me first say that as a believer what you are to wait for is the fuller manifestation of the power of the Spirit within you. On the resurrection morning Jesus breathed on His disciples and said, "Receive the Holy Spirit." They were to wait for the full baptism of fire and of power. Yes, as God's child you have the Holy Spirit. (Study the passages in the Epistles addressed to believers full of failings and sins: 1 Corinthians 3:1–3, 16; 6:19–20; Galatians 3:2–3; 4:6.) Begin in simple faith in God's Word to cultivate this quiet assurance: The Holy Spirit is dwelling within you. But if you are not faithful in what you have, you cannot expect more. Each time you enter your closet to speak with God, first remember that the Spirit is within you as the Spirit of prayer. You are a temple of the Holy Spirit.

You are in position for taking the second step: Ask God to grant you the work of His Holy Spirit. The Spirit is in God and also in you. Ask your Father that His almighty Spirit may come from Him in greater life and power so that He may work more mightily in you. As you ask this on the ground of the promises, believe that He hears and that He will do it. You must not look to see whether you *feel* anything. You are to believe, rest in what God is going to do, even is doing now, though you may not feel it.

And then comes the waiting. Wait on the Lord; wait for His Spirit. Be still before God and allow Him to quicken in you the assurance that He will grant the Spirit's work in you. We are a holy priesthood to offer up spiritual sacrifice. Under the old covenant, the slaying of the sacrifice was an essential part of the service. In each sacrifice you bring there must be a surrender of self and its power. As you wait before God He interprets your silence as confession that you have nothing—no wisdom or strength to pray or to work aright. Waiting is an expression of need, of emptiness. All through the Christian life these are contrasted: poverty and weakness on our part, all-sufficiency and strength on God's part. It is in waiting before God that the soul recognizes its own deficiency and is lifted up into the divine assurance that God accepts its sacrifice and will fulfill all its needs and desires.

After the soul has waited upon God, it must go forward to the day's walk or task, leaving behind the work of petition in the faith that God will see to the fulfillment of His promise. If you give yourself to prayer after waiting for the Spirit, or to the reading of the Word, do it in faith that the Holy Spirit guides your prayer and your thoughts. If your experience appears to prove that nothing has happened, be assured that this is simply to lead you onward to a simpler faith and a more entire surrender. You have become so accustomed to worship in the power of human understanding and the carnal mind that true spiritual worship does not come at once. But wait: "He commanded them . . . to wait" (Acts 1:4). Keep up the waiting disposition in your daily life and work. "On You I wait all the day" (Psalm 25:5).

It is to the triune God we speak; the Holy Spirit brings Him near and unites us to Him. Renew your faith each day, and as you are able to do it, extend your exercise of waiting upon God. The multitude of words and fervent feelings in prayer are often more of a hindrance than a help. God's work in you must become deeper, more spiritual, more directly wrought of God himself. Wait for the promise in all its fullness. Do not count the time lost that you give to the expression of humility and emptiness, of faith and expectation, of surrender to the authority of the Spirit. Pentecost was meant to be the proof of what the exalted Jesus does for His church from His throne. The ten days' waiting was intended to be the position before the throne that secures the Pentecostal blessing. The promise of the Father is certain. It is Jesus from whom you have it. The Spirit himself is already working in you. His full indwelling and guidance is your portion as His child. Keep the charge of your Lord! Wait on God, wait for the Spirit. "Wait, I say, on the Lord. Blessed are all they who wait for Him."

Blessed Father, from your beloved Son we have heard your promise. In a pouring forth that is divine and never-ceasing, the river of the water of life flows from under the throne of God and the Lamb. Your Spirit flows down to quicken our thirsty souls. For we have not heard, neither has the eye seen, O God, beside you, what He has prepared for them that love Him, for them that wait for Him.

We have heard His command to wait for the promise. We thank you for what has already been fulfilled to us of it. But our souls long for the full possession, the fullness of the blessing of Christ. Father, teach us to wait on you, daily watching at the posts of your doors.

Teach us each day as we draw near to you to wait for

Him. In the sacrifice of our own wisdom and our will, in the fear of the workings of our own nature, may we learn to walk humbly before you so that your Spirit might work with power. And teach us that as the life of self is laid down before you day by day, the holy life that flows from the throne will rise in power and our worship will be in spirit and in truth. Amen.

Summary

1. The disciples were not to proceed to do their work in the faith of the promise that the Spirit would be given: They were to wait until they could joyfully testify and prove that Christ in heaven had given His Spirit within them.

2. We are not to look back for our Pentecost. The Pentecost of Acts is given to make the church of Christ acquainted with the privileges belonging to this dispensation. The Spirit of God comes as the rain, which must come again and again, and as the wind, which must blow again and again.

3. *Waiting*—it is the all-comprehensive word to indicate the attitude of the disciples toward the promise of the Father. Waiting includes the denial of self, its wisdom and strength; separation from all else; surrender and preparedness for all the Spirit would claim; joyful faith in what Christ is, and confident expectation of what He is going to do. *Wait!* It is the one final condition imposed by the ascending Lord for the fulfillment of the promise.

4. Let waiting be the deep undergirding of the daily life in relation to the Spirit for each one who knows that the Spirit is in him and who longs to be strengthened by

Him. Let it be the attitude of the church as she expects her Lord, in answer to her prayer, to manifest His power in the world. He charged them to wait, to tarry until they were clothed with power from on high.

5. As Christ is the fulfillment of the law and the end of the law, so the Spirit is the complement, the fulfillment, and the confirmation of the Gospel. All that Christ did would have profited us nothing if the Holy Spirit did not come into our hearts and bring it all home to us.

Chapter 14

The Spirit of Power

But you shall be baptized with the Holy Spirit not many days from now. You shall receive power when the Holy Spirit has come upon you; and you shall be witnesses to Me in Jerusalem, and in all Judea and Samaria, and to the end of the earth.

Acts 1:5, 8

Behold, I send the Promise of My Father upon you; but tarry in the city of Jerusalem until you are endued with power from on high.

Luke 24:49

The disciples had heard from John of the baptism of the Spirit. Jesus had spoken to them about the Father giving the Spirit to them that ask Him and of the Spirit of their Father speaking through them. And on the last night he spoke of the Spirit dwelling in them, witnessing through them, coming to convince the world of sin. All these thoughts of what the coming of the Holy Spirit would mean was connected in their minds with the work they would have to do and the power they would have for it. When our Lord summed up all His teaching in the promise "You shall receive power when the Holy Spirit has come upon you; and you shall be witnesses to Me," it must have been to them the summing up of what they looked for—a new divine power for the new divine work of being witnesses of the crucified and risen Christ.

This was in perfect harmony with all they had seen in Scripture of the Spirit's work: In the days before the flood God strove with men to repent. For the ministry of Moses, He equipped him as well as the seventy who received of His Spirit for the work of ruling and guiding Israel, and He gave wisdom to those who built God's house. In the days of the judges He gave the power to fight and conquer their enemies. In the times of the kings and prophets He gave boldness to testify against sin and power to proclaim the coming redemption. Every mention of the Spirit in the Old Testament is connected with the honor and kingdom of God and the equipping for service in it. In the great prophecy of the Messiah, with which the Son of God opened His ministry at Nazareth, His being anointed with the Spirit had the sole purpose of bringing deliverance to the captives and gladness to the sorrowing. To the mind of the disciples, as students of the Old Testament and followers of Christ Jesus, the promise of the Spirit could have but one meaning: power for the great work they had to do for their Lord when He ascended the throne. All that the Spirit would be to them personally in His work of comforting, teaching, sanctifying the soul, and glorifying Jesus were but a means to an end—their anointing with power for the service of their departed Lord.

My prayer is that the church of Christ today would understand this. All prayers for the guiding and encouraging influence of the Holy Spirit in the children of God ought to have this as their aim: power to witness for Christ and effectively serve in reaching the world for Him. Waste of power is a cause for regret to those who witness it. The economy of power is one of the objectives of every organization and industry. The Holy Spirit is the power of God, the power of God's redemption as it comes from the throne of Him to whom all power has been given. Would God waste this power on those who seek it only for their own good? The Holy Spirit is the power from on high for carrying on the work for which Jesus sacrificed His throne and His life. The essential condition for receiving that power is that we are ready and willing to do the work the Spirit has come to accomplish.

My witnesses. These words contain a divine and inexhaustible wealth of meaning. They are the object of the Spirit's work, the work for which nothing less than His divine power is needed; the work by which our weakness is made strong. There is nothing as effective as an honest witness. Even the learned eloquence of a lawyer must be convinced by it. There is nothing so simple: telling what we have seen and heard. It was the great work of Jesus himself. He was born and came into the world that He might bear witness to the truth. And yet as simple as it appears, the almighty power of the Spirit is needed to make us effective witnesses of Jesus. It is what He was sent to do. If we are to witness of Jesus as He reigns in heaven, in the power of the eternal life and power of the world to come, we need nothing less than the power of the heavenly life to strengthen the testimony of our lips and life.

The Holy Spirit makes us witnesses because He is a witness. Jesus said, "He shall witness of me." On the day of Pentecost, when Peter preached that Christ, when He had ascended into heaven, had received from the Father the Holy Spirit and had poured Him forth, he spoke of what he knew: the Holy Spirit witnessed to him and in him of the glory of his exalted Lord. It was this witness of the Spirit to the reality of Christ's power and presence that made him bold and strong to speak before the council: "God has raised this Jesus to life, and we are all witnesses of the fact. Exalted to the right hand of God, he has received from the Father the promised Holy Spirit and has poured out what you now see and hear. God has made this Jesus, whom you crucified, both Lord and Christ" (Acts 2:32–33, 36). When the Holy Spirit, in a divine life and power, witnesses to us what Jesus is at the present moment in His glory, our witness will be in His power. We may know all that the Gospels record and all that Scripture further teaches of the person and work of Jesus; we may even speak from past experience of what we once knew of the power of Jesus. This is not the witness of power that is promised here and that will have effect in the world. It is the presence of the Spirit at the present moment—witnessing to the presence of the personal Jesus—that gives our witness that breath of life from heaven that makes it mighty through God to the casting down of strongholds. You can witness to as much of Jesus as the Holy Spirit is witnessing to you in life and truth.

The baptism of power, the enduement of power, is sometimes spoken of and sought after as a special gift. If Paul asked distinctly for the Ephesians, who had been sealed with the Holy Spirit, that the Father would still give them "the spirit of wisdom" (Ephesians 1:17), we cannot be wrong in praying for "the spirit of power." He who searches the hearts knows what the mind of the Spirit is, and He will not give according to the perfection of our words, but the Spirit-breathed desire of our hearts. Or let us use the other prayer of Paul (Ephesians 3:16), and plead that He would grant us "to be strengthened with might through his Spirit in the inner man." However we formulate our prayer, one thing is certain: It is in unceasing prayer, it is in bowing our knees, it is in waiting on God that from Him will come what we ask, whether it is the spirit of power or the power of the Spirit. The Spirit is never separate from God; in all His moving about and working He is still the innermost being of God. It is God himself who, according to the riches of His glory, is mighty to do above what we ask or think, who will in Christ clothe us with the power of the Spirit.

In seeking for this power of the Spirit, let us note the mode in which He works. There is one mistake we must watch for: always expecting to *feel* the power when it works. Scripture links power and weakness in a wonderful way, not as succeeding each other, but as existing together. In summary, Paul said, "I was with you in weakness; my preaching was in power. When I am weak, then am I strong." (See 1 Corinthians 2:3–5; 2 Corinthians 4:7, 16; 6:10; 12:10; 13:4.) The power is the power of God, given to faith; and faith grows strong in the dark. The Holy Spirit hides himself in the weak things that God has chosen, that flesh might not glory in His presence. Spiritual power can be known only by the Spirit of faith. The more distinctly we feel and confess our weakness and believe in the power dwelling within us, ready to work as the need arises, the more confidently we may expect its divine operation even when nothing is felt. Christians lose much not only by not waiting for the power, but by waiting in the wrong way. Seek to combine faithful and ready obedience to every call of duty, however small your power appears to be, with a deep, dependent waiting, and expecting power from on high. Let your intervals of rest and communion be the exercise of prayer and faith in the power of God dwelling in you and waiting to work through you. Your time spent will bring the proof that by faith, through weakness, we are made strong.

Let us also see and make no mistake about *the condition* of the working of this divine power. He who would command nature must first obey her. It does not take much grace to long and ask for power, even the power of the Spirit. Who would not be glad to have power? Many pray earnestly for power for their work and do not receive it because they do not accept the only position through which power comes. We want to get possession of power and use it. God wants to get possession of us and use us. If we give ourselves to God's power to rule in us, His power will give itself to us to rule through us. Unconditional submission and obedience to God's power in our inner life is the one condition for our being clothed with it. God gives the Spirit to the obedient. "Power belongs unto God" and remains His forever. If you would have His power work in you, bow before the holy presence that dwells in you, that asks your surrender to His guidance even in the smallest things. Walk humbly in holy fear, lest in anything you should fail to know or do His will. Live as one given to a power that has complete control, entire possession of your inmost being.

Let the Spirit and His power have possession of you and you will know His power working in you.

Let us be clear as to *the object* of this power, the work it is to do. People are careful to economize power and to channel it where it can do its work most effectively. God does not give this power for our own enjoyment or to save us from trouble and effort. He gives it for one purpose—to glorify His Son. Those who in their weakness are faithful to this one object, who in obedience and by their testimony prove to God that they are ready at any cost to glorify Him, they will receive power from on high. God seeks men and women whom He can clothe with His power. The church is looking for these, wondering at the futility of so much of its ministry and worship. The world waits for it, to be convinced that God is indeed in the midst of His people. The perishing millions are crying for deliverance, and the power of God is waiting to deliver them. Let us not be content to pray to God to visit and to bless them, or to try to do what we can in our own strength. Let us give ourselves wholly and undividedly to live as faithful witnesses for Christ and believe that His Spirit is within us to reach a dying world.

Father, I thank you for the wonderful provision you have made for your children—that out of weakness they should be made strong, and that in their faltering your mighty Spirit should be glorified. I thank you for the Holy Spirit, the Spirit of power that comes to make Jesus, to whom all power is given, present with His church, and to make His disciples the witnesses of that presence.

I ask you, Father, to teach me that I have as much power as I have the living Jesus and that I am not to look for it to come so that I can see it or feel it. It is divine strength for my human weakness so that the glory may be yours alone. May I learn to receive it in faith that allows the Lord Jesus to do His work in the midst of my weakness. Make the Holy Spirit so present with me that my witness may be of Him alone.

I desire, my Father, to submit my whole being to your holy power. I would bow before your rule every day and all day. I would be your servant and humble myself to obey your most difficult commands. Father, let your power rule in me that I may be made fit for your use. My one goal in life is that your Son will receive all the honor and the glory. Amen.

Summary

1. There is a presence in the church of Christ as omnipotent and divine as Christ himself when He was on earth, rather as He is now on the throne of power. As the church wakes up to believe this and rises out of the dust to put on her beautiful garments, as she waits on her Lord to be "clothed with power from on high," her witness for Christ will be in living power. She will prove that her almighty Lord is in her.

2. This "clothing with power from on high," this "receiving the power of the Holy Spirit," takes place in a way contrary to our natural expectations. It is divine power working in weakness. The sense of weakness is not taken away: the power is not given as something we possess. We only have the power as we have the Lord himself. He exerts the power in and through our weakness.

3. Our greatest danger is waiting for the sight or sense of power. Our one need is faith that spiritually recognizes the mighty Lord as present and knows that He will work

in our weakness. Being clothed with power, or receiving the power, is appropriating the Lord Jesus, receiving Him in faith, so that our souls rejoice in His hidden presence, and know that His power is working in our weakness.

4. As the character of a body depends upon the various particles of which it is composed, so the power of the church of Christ will be decided by the state of its individual members. The Holy Spirit cannot work mightily through the church of God in the world until the mass of individual believers give themselves wholly to their Lord to be filled with His Spirit. Let us labor and pray toward this end.

5. A personal power, with a will and a purpose, has control within me, ready to work His will into mine in all things. Another will than my own, now ruling in the depths of my being, is to be waited upon. As I submit and obey, His power will work through me. I live under the power of another.

6. "For I also am a man under authority, having soldiers under me. And I say to this one, 'Go,' and he goes" (Matthew 8:9). The man who is himself under a higher power has that power to rule those under him. To lead others effectively, I must first be under the highest power.

Chapter 15

The Outpouring
of the Spirit

*When the Day of Pentecost had fully come, they were all
with one accord in one place. And they were all filled with
the Holy Spirit and began to speak with other tongues,
as the Spirit gave them utterance.*

Acts 2:1, 4

In the outpouring of the Holy Spirit the work of Christ is
culminated. The awesome mystery of the incarnation in
Bethlehem, the great redemption accomplished on Calvary,
the revelation of Christ as the Son of God in the power of
eternal life through the resurrection, His entrance into
glory in the ascension—these are all preliminary stages;
their goal and their crown was the coming of the Holy
Spirit. The day had fully come. Pentecost is the last and
greatest of the Christian feasts; in it the others find their
realization and fulfillment. It is because the church has
scarcely acknowledged this and has not seen the glory of
Pentecost as the highest glory of the Father and the Son that

the Holy Spirit has not been able to fully reveal and glorify the Son in her. Let us examine what Pentecost means.

God made man in His own image and after His likeness with the purpose that he should become like himself. Man was to be the temple for God's dwelling; he was to be the home for God's rest. The closest and most intimate union, the indwelling of love, was what the Holy One longed for. What was inadequately set forth in type in the temple in Israel became divine reality in Jesus of Nazareth. God found a man in whom He could rest, whose whole being was open to the rule of His will and the fellowship of His love. In Him there was human nature possessed by the divine Spirit; God would have all men to be such. And such all would be who accepted Jesus as their life. His death was to remove the curse and power of sin and make it possible for them to receive His Spirit. His resurrection was the entrance of human nature, free from all weakness of the flesh, into the divine Spirit-life. His ascension was admittance as man into the very glory of God, the participation by human nature of perfect fellowship with God in glory in the unity of the Spirit. And yet with all this the work was not complete. The primary thing was still lacking. How could the Father dwell in men as He had dwelt in Christ? This was the question to which Pentecost gives the answer.

Out of the depths of the Godhead, the Holy Spirit is sent forth in a new character and a new power, such as He never had before. In creation and nature He came forth from God as the Spirit of life. In the creation of man particularly He acted as the power in which His godlikeness was grounded, and after the fall of man still testified for God. In Israel He appeared as the Spirit of the theocracy, distinctly inspiring and equipping certain men for their work. In Jesus Christ He came as the Spirit of the Father, given to Him without measure, and abiding in Him. All these are manifestations, in different degrees, of one and the same Spirit. But now there comes the last, long-promised, entirely new manifestation of the divine Spirit. The Spirit that dwelt in Jesus Christ, and in His life of obedience has taken up His human spirit into perfect fellowship and unity with himself, is now the Spirit of the exalted God-man. As the man Christ Jesus enters the glory of God and the full fellowship of that Spirit-life in which God dwells, He receives from the Father the right to send forth His Spirit into His disciples, that is, in the Spirit to descend himself and dwell in them. The Spirit comes in a new power, which before had not been possible because Jesus had not yet been crucified or glorified. He comes as the very Spirit of the glorified Jesus. The work of the Son, the longing of the Father, receives its fulfillment. Man's heart has become the home of God.

I said that Pentecost is the greatest of the church's feasts. The mystery of Bethlehem is indeed incomprehensible and glorious, but when once I believe it, there is nothing that appears impossible. That a pure, holy body should be formed for the Son of God by the power of the Holy Spirit, and that in that body the Spirit should dwell, is indeed a miracle of divine power. But that the same Spirit should now come and dwell in the bodies of sinful men, that in them also the Father should take up His residence, this is a mystery of grace that passes all understanding. But this is the blessing Pentecost brings and receives. The entrance of the Son of God into the likeness of our flesh in Bethlehem, into the curse and death of sin in our place, in human nature as first-begotten from the dead into the power of eternal life, and His entrance into the very glory of the Father—these were but the preparatory steps: Here is the consummation for which all the rest was accomplished. The word now begins to be fulfilled: "Behold, the tabernacle of God is with men, and He will dwell with them, and they shall be His people" (Revelation 21:3).

It is only in the light of all that preceded Pentecost—of the great sacrifice that God did not consider too great so that He might dwell with sinful men—that the narrative of the outpouring of the Spirit can be understood. It is the earthly reflection of Christ's exaltation in heaven, the participation He gives to His friends of the glory He now has with the Father. To be understood fully we need a spiritual enlightening. In the story that is so simply told, the deepest mysteries of the kingdom unfold, and the title deeds are given to the church of her holy heritage until her Lord's return. What the Spirit is to be to *believers* and the church, to the *ministers* of the Word and their work, and to the unbelieving *world,* are the three main emphases.

First, Christ promised to His disciples that in the Helper (the Comforter) He would again come to them. During His life on earth, His personal manifested presence, revealing the unseen Father, was the Father's gift to men—the one thing the disciples longed for and needed. This was to be their portion in greater power than before. Christ had entered glory with this very purpose, that now, in a divine way, "He might fill all things," particularly the members of His body, with His glorified life. When the Holy Spirit came, He came as a personal life within them. Previously

He had been a life apart from them, outside their natural life. The very Spirit of God's own Son, as He had lived and loved, obeyed and died, was raised and glorified, and was now to become a vibrant life within them. The wondrous transaction that had taken place in heaven, in the placing of their Lord on the throne of heaven, this the Holy Spirit came to be witness of, even to communicate it and maintain it within them as a heavenly reality. It is indeed no wonder that as the Holy Spirit came down from the Father through the glorified Son, their whole nature was filled to overflowing with the joy and power of heaven, with the presence of Jesus, and their lips overflowed with the praise of the wonderful works of God.

Such was the birth of the church of Christ and such must be its growth and strength. The first element of the succession of the church at Pentecost is a membership baptized with the Holy Spirit and fire—every heart filled with the experience of the presence of the glorified Lord, every tongue and life witnessing to the wonderful work God has done in raising Jesus to glory and then filling His disciples with that same glory. It is not so much the baptism of power for our preachers that we seek; rather, it is that every individual member of Christ's body may know, possess, and witness to the presence of an indwelling Christ through the Holy Spirit. This is what will draw the attention of the world and compel a confession to the power of Jesus.

Second, it was amid the interest and the questionings that the sight of this joyous praising company of believers awakened in the multitude that Peter stood up to preach. The story of Pentecost teaches us the true position of the ministry and the secret of its power. A church full of the

Holy Spirit is the power of God to awaken the careless and attract honest, earnest hearts. It is to such an audience— awakened by the testimony of believers—that the preaching will come with power. It is out of such a church of men and women full of the Holy Spirit that Spirit-led preachers will rise up, bold and free, to point to every believer as a living witness to the truth of their preaching and the power of their Lord.

Peter's preaching is a most remarkable example of what all Holy Spirit preaching will be. He preaches Christ from the Scriptures. In contrast with the thoughts of men, who had rejected Christ, He sets forth the thoughts of God, who had sent Christ, who delighted in Him, and had now exalted Him at His right hand. All preaching in the power of the Holy Spirit will do the same. The Spirit is the Spirit of Christ, the Spirit of His personal life, taking possession of our personality and witnessing with our spirit to what Christ has won for us. The Spirit has come for the very purpose of continuing the work Christ began on earth, of making men partakers of His redemption and His life. It could not be otherwise; the Spirit always witnesses to Christ. He did so in the Scriptures; He does so in the believer; the believer's testimony will always be according to Scripture. The Spirit in Christ, the Spirit in Scripture, the Spirit in the church; as long as this threefold cord is inter- twined, it cannot be broken.

Third, the effect of this preaching was a marvelous thing, but not more so than was to be expected. The pres- ence and power of Jesus were a reality in the company of the disciples. The power from the throne filled Peter. The vision he had of Christ exalted at the right hand of God was such a spiritual reality that power emanated from him. As his preaching reached its application: "Know assuredly that God has made this Jesus, whom you crucified, both Lord and Christ" (Acts 2:36), thousands bowed in brokenness of spirit, ready to acknowledge the crucified one as their Lord and Savior. The Spirit had come to the disciples and through them convinced the hearers of their unbelief. The penitent inquirers listened to the command to repent and believe, and they received the gift of the Holy Spirit. The greater works that Christ had promised to do through the disciples, He had done. In one moment, lifelong prejudice and bitter hatred gave way to surrender, love, and adoration. From the glorified Lord, power filled Peter, and from him that power went out to conquer sin and to save the sinner.

Pentecost is the glorious sunrise of "that day," the first of "those days" of which the prophets and our Lord had so often spoken, the promise and the pledge of what the history of the church was meant to be. It is universally admitted that the church has less than fulfilled her destiny, that even now, after twenty centuries, she has not risen to the height of her glorious privileges. Even when she strives to accept her calling, to witness for her Lord unto the ends of the earth, she does not do it in the faith of the Spirit of Pentecost and the possession of His mighty power. Instead of regarding Pentecost as a sunrise, she too often speaks and acts as if it had been noonday, from which the light must soon begin to fade. Let the church return to Pentecost, and Pentecost will return to her. The Spirit of God cannot take possession of believers beyond their capacity to receive Him. The promise is waiting; the Spirit is available in all

His fullness. Our capacity needs to be enlarged. While believers continue with one accord in praise, love, and prayer, holding fast the promise in faith, and gaze upon the exalted Lord in the confidence that He will make himself known in power in the midst of His people, it is at the footstool of the throne that Pentecost comes. Jesus Christ is still Lord of all, crowned with power and glory. His longing to reveal His presence in His disciples—to make them share the glory-life in which He dwells—is as fresh and full as when He first ascended the throne. Let us take our place at the footstool. Let us yield ourselves in expectant faith to be filled with the Holy Spirit and to testify of Him. Let the indwelling Christ be our life, our strength, our testimony. Out of such a church, Spirit-filled leaders will rise with the power that will make Christ's enemies bow at His feet.

O Lord God, we worship before the throne on which the Son is seated with you, crowned with glory and honor. We thank and bless you that He in whom you delight belongs as much to earth as to heaven, as much to us as to you. O God, we adore you; we praise your holy name.

We ask that you reveal to your church how our blessed Head considers us His own body, sharing with Him in His life, His power, and His glory, and how the Holy Spirit, as the bearer of that life and power, is waiting to reveal it within us. Oh, that your people might be awakened to know what the Holy Spirit means: the true presence of the glorified Lord within as the clothing with power from on high for their work on earth. May all your people learn to gaze on their exalted King until their whole being is given to Him and His Spirit fills them to capacity.

Our Father, our plea, in the name of Jesus, is that you revive your church. Make every believer a temple of the Holy Spirit. Make every church—its believing members—a consecrated company that testifies to a present Christ; ever waiting for the fullness of the power from on high. Make every preacher of the Word a minister of the Spirit. Let Pentecost throughout the earth be the sign that Jesus reigns, the redeemed are His body, His Spirit works, and one day every knee shall bow before Him. Amen.

Summary

1. When Jesus returned to heaven, He could not bear the thought that His returning to glory should cause the slightest separation between himself and His faithful followers. The mission of the Spirit was to secure and give to them His promised presence. This is the blessedness of the Spirit's work; this makes Him the power of God in us for service.

2. The perfect health of a body means the health of every member. The healthy work of the Spirit in the church requires the health of every individual believer. Let us pray to this end that the presence of Christ, by the indwelling Spirit in every believer, will make our seasons of worship a repetition of Pentecost: the waiting, receptive, worshiping company on earth met by the Spirit of Christ from heaven.

Chapter 16

The Holy Spirit
and Missions

*Now in the church that was at Antioch there were certain
prophets and teachers. . . . As they ministered to the Lord
and fasted, the Holy Spirit said, "Now separate to Me
Barnabas and Saul for the work to which I have called
them." Then, having fasted and prayed, and laid hands
on them, they sent them away. So, being sent out
by the Holy Spirit, they went down to Seleucia,
and from there they sailed to Cyprus.*

Acts 13:1–4

It has been said that the Acts of the Apostles might well
have been called the Acts of the Exalted Lord or the Acts of
the Holy Spirit. Christ's parting promise "You shall receive
power when the Holy Spirit is come upon you; and you
shall be witnesses to Me in Jerusalem, and in all Judea and
Samaria, and to the end of the earth" (Acts 1:8) was indeed
one of those divine seed-words in which is contained the
kingdom of heaven in the power of an infinite growth, with

the certainty of its manifestation and the prophecy of its fulfillment. In the book of the Acts we have the way traced in which the promise received its initial fulfillment on its way from Jerusalem to Rome. It gives us the divine record of the coming, dwelling, and working of the Holy Spirit as the power given to Christ's disciples to witness for Him before Jews and heathen, and of the triumph of the name of Christ in Antioch and Rome as the centers for the conquest of the uttermost parts of the earth. The book reveals, as with a light from heaven, that the one aim and purpose of the descent of the Spirit from our glorified Lord in heaven to His disciples—to reveal in them His presence, His guidance, and His power—was to equip them to be His witnesses to the uttermost parts of the earth. Mission to the lost is the ultimate goal of the Spirit.

In the passage we have as our text, we have the first record of the part the church is called to take in the work of missions. In the preaching of Philip at Samaria and Peter at Caesarea we have the examples of individual men exercising their function of ministry, under the leading of the Spirit, among those who were not Jews. In the preaching of the men of Cyprus and Cyrene to the Greeks at Antioch we have the divine instinct of the Spirit of love and life leading men to open new paths where the leaders of the church had not yet gone. But this guidance of the Spirit in separating particular individuals was now to become part of the organization of the church, and the whole community of believers was to be educated in taking its share in the work for which the Spirit had specifically come to earth. If Acts 2 is of importance in giving us the empowerment of the church for her work in Jerusalem, Acts 13 is of no less importance in the church's being set apart for the work of missions. We cannot praise God enough for the deepening interest in missions in our day. If our interest is to be permanent and personal, if it is to be expressed in enthusiastic love and devotion to our blessed Lord and the lost He came to save, and if it is to be fruitful in raising the work of the church to the true level of Pentecostal power, we must learn the lesson of Antioch. Mission work must find its initiative and its power in the distinct and direct acknowledgment of the guidance of the Holy Spirit.

It has often been said that true mission work has always been born of a revival of spiritual life in the church. The Holy Spirit's quickening work stirs us up to new devotion to the blessed Lord whom He reveals and dedication to the lost for whom He died. It is in such a condition of heart and mind that the urging of the Spirit is heard. So it was at Antioch. There were certain prophets and teachers there who spent part of their time ministering to the Lord in fasting and prayer. With the public service to God in the church, they combined a spirit of separation from the world. They felt the need of close and continued fellowship while waiting for His orders from heaven. They believed that the Spirit that dwelt in them could not have free and full reign except while they maintained direct communion with Him. Such was their state of mind and habit of life when the Holy Spirit revealed to them that He had called two of their number to a special ministry and asked them to separate these, in the presence of the whole church, for that work.

The law of the kingdom has not changed. It is still the Holy Spirit who is in charge of all mission work. He will reveal His will in the appointment of tasks and selection of those who are waiting on the Lord. When once the Holy Spirit at any time has taught men of faith and prayer to undertake His work, it is more likely that others, admiring and approving what they do, will see the harmony of their conduct with Scripture and desire to follow their example. And yet the real power of the Spirit's guiding and working as well as the personal love and devotion to Jesus as Lord may be present only to a small degree. It is because so much interest in the missionary cause is attained in this way that there is often difficulty in convincing its supporters of its genuine need and validity. The command of the Lord is known as it is recorded in the Bible; the living voice of the Spirit, who reveals the Lord in living presence and power, is not always heard. It is not enough that Christians are stirred and urged to take a greater interest in missions, to pray or to give more financially. There is a more urgent need. In the life of the individual, the indwelling of the Holy Spirit and the presence and rule of the Lord of glory that He maintains, must again become the primary goal of the Christian life. In the fellowship of the church we must learn to wait more earnestly for the Holy Spirit's guidance in the selection of workers and fields of labor and in awakening interest and seeking support. The mission that originates in prayer and waiting on the Spirit can expect His power.

Let no one imagine that when we speak this way we intend to lead Christians away from the practical aspect of the work that must be done. There is much that needs cooperation and diligence to accomplish a work in another country or even another city. Information must be circulated, people must be recruited, funds must be raised, sufficient prayer must be offered; committees and directors must meet, consult, and decide. All of this is necessary. But it will be done well, and as a service well-pleasing to the Master, only in the measure in which it is done in the power of the Holy Spirit. The Spirit has called the church to be missionary-minded, to inspire and empower Christ's disciples to spread the gospel to the ends of the earth.

The origin, the progress, the success of missions are His. It is He who awakens in the hearts of believers the zeal for the honor of the Lord, the compassion for the souls of the lost, the faith in His promises, the willing obedience to His commands by which such a ministry grows and succeeds. It is He who draws up a united effort, who calls forth workers to go out, who opens the doors and prepares the hearts of those who will hear the Word. It is He who at length blesses the harvest, and in places where Satan's power is established, gathers around the redeemed of the Lord to break down the strongholds. Missions are the special work of the Holy Spirit. No one can expect to be filled with the Spirit if he is not willing to be used in some way in the harvest. And no one who wishes to work or pray for missions needs to fear his own weakness or poverty. The Holy Spirit is the power that can equip him to take his divinely appointed place in the work of the gospel. Let every one who prays for missions, who longs for a larger missionary spirit in the church, pray first that in every one who has a part, the power of the indwelling Spirit may have full influence and control.

The sending out of laborers is equally the work of the church and of the Spirit. This is the common connection.

But there are some who are sent out by the Holy Spirit alone, amid the opposition or indifference of the church. Contrarily, some go out under the church without the blessing and sanction of the Holy Spirit. Blessed by far is the church whose missionary effort the Spirit originates, where He is allowed to lead and guide and send. After ten days' praying and waiting on earth, the Spirit descended in fire: This was the birth of the church at Jerusalem. After ministering and fasting, waiting and praying, the Spirit sent forth Barnabas and Saul: This was at Antioch the consecration of the church to be a missionary church.

I would say to any missionary who reads this text in his home away from home: "Be encouraged, brother, sister! The Holy Spirit, who is the mighty power of God, who is the presence of Jesus within you, is with you and in you and for you. The work is His: Depend on Him, yield to Him, wait for Him; the work is His and He will accomplish it.

To every Christian, whether mission director, prayer supporter, financial contributor, or in any other way working to hasten the coming of the kingdom, "Be encouraged." From the time of waiting and the baptism of the Spirit received, the first disciples went forth until they reached Antioch. There they paused, prayed, fasted, and then continued to Rome and the regions beyond. Let us from these, our brethren, learn the secret of power. Let us call on every Christian who would be a friend of missions to come with us and be filled with the Spirit, whose work is the work of missions. Let us lift up a clear witness that the need of the church and the world is a group of believers who can testify to an indwelling Christ by the Spirit and prove His power to work. Let us gather together in the antechamber of the King's presence—the waiting at Jerusalem, the ministering and fasting at Antioch. The Spirit still comes as He did then. He still moves and sends out; He is still strong to convict of sin and to reveal Jesus Christ, and to bring multitudes to His feet. He waits for us: Let us wait on Him and be ready to welcome His call.

O God, you sent your Son to be the Savior of the world. You gave Him power over all flesh that He might grant eternal life to as many as you have given Him. And you poured out your Spirit upon all flesh, commissioning as many as received Him to make known the glorious news. In the love and power in which your Spirit was sent forth, He sends those who yield themselves to Him to be the instruments of His power. We thank you for your complete and all-encompassing salvation.

We stand amazed and ashamed at the idleness and neglect of your church in not fulfilling her divine commission. We are humbled at our slowness of heart to perceive and believe what your Son promised, to obey His will and finish His work. We cry to you, our God! Visit your church and let your Spirit, the Spirit of missions, fill your children.

O Father, I dedicate myself afresh to you to live and labor, to pray and travail, to sacrifice and suffer if need be for your kingdom. I accept anew in faith the wonderful gift of the Holy Spirit, the very Spirit of Christ, and yield myself to His indwelling. I humbly plead with you to allow me and all your children to be so mightily strengthened by the Holy Spirit that Christ may possess our heart and life, and that our one desire will be that the whole earth be filled with His glory. Amen.

Summary

1. "Sent forth by the Holy Spirit." The Holy Spirit was *sent* by the Son from the Father to continue His work on earth. He accomplishes this by sending forth His people into the harvest. The mission of the Spirit was meant by God to give the church the Spirit of missions. His outpouring is upon all flesh. He cannot rest until all have heard of Christ.

2. A missionary spirit is Christ's Spirit—the pure flame of His love for souls burning brightly enough in us to make us first willing, then longing to go anywhere, and to suffer any deprivation, in order to seek and find the lost in the areas of the world that are unreached with the gospel.

3. Is it true that we belong to Christ? If we do not have the Spirit of Christ, we do not belong to Him. We know that the Spirit of the Savior was a spirit of self-sacrifice for the salvation of the world. We must apply the test to our own hearts.

4. Jesus sent the Holy Spirit to take possession of our hearts that He might live therein and work in and through us, even as the Father worked in and through Him. I will wait on the Lord until my soul is filled with the assurance that the Spirit dwells in me, His very presence. To this Spirit I yield myself, even as the disciples did. They saw with Christ's eyes, they felt with His heart, they worked with His energy; they had His Spirit. And we have His Spirit, too.

5. On the second to his last birthday, Livingstone wrote: "My Jesus, my king, my life, my all. I again dedicate my whole self to you." He died on his knees, with his face buried in his hands, praying.

Chapter 17

The Newness
of the Spirit

But now we have been delivered from the law, having died
to what we were held by, so that we should serve in the
newness of the Spirit and not in the oldness of the letter.

Romans 7:6

But if you are led by the Spirit, you are not under the law.

Galatians 5:18

The work of the indwelling Spirit is to glorify Christ and to reveal Him to us. Corresponding to Christ's threefold office of prophet, priest, and king we find that the work of the indwelling Spirit in the believer has three aspects: enlightening, sanctifying, and strengthening. Of the enlightening, Christ particularly speaks in His farewell discourse, when He promises the Spirit as the Spirit of truth, who will bear witness of Him, will guide into all truth, and will take of Christ and declare it unto us. In the epistles to the Romans and the Galatians, His work of sanctifying is especially prominent: This was what was needed in churches so recently brought out of paganism. In the epistles to the Corinthians, where wisdom was especially prized and sought, the two aspects are combined; they are taught that the Spirit can only enlighten as He sanctifies (1 Corinthians 2, 3:1–3, 16; 2 Corinthians 3). In the Acts of the Apostles, as we might expect, His strengthening for service is in the forefront; as the promised Spirit of power, He equips for a bold testimony in the midst of persecution and difficulty.

In the epistle to the church at Rome, the capital of the world, Paul was called of God to give a full and systematic exposition of His gospel and the plan of redemption. In this the work of the Holy Spirit must have an important place. In giving his text or theme "The just shall live by faith" (Romans 1:17), he paves the way for what he was to expound: that through faith both righteousness and life would come. In the first part of his argument (Romans 6:11), he teaches what the righteousness of faith is. He then proceeds (vv. 12–21) to prove how this righteousness is rooted in our living connection with the second Adam and in a justification of life. In the individual (vv. 1–13) this life comes through accepting Christ's death to sin and His life in God as ours and the willing surrender (6:14–23) to be servants of God and of righteousness. Proceeding to show that in Christ we are not only dead to sin but also to the law—the strength of sin—he comes naturally to the new law that His gospel brings to take the place of the old, the law of the Spirit of life in Christ Jesus.

We know how an impression is strengthened by contrast. Just as the apostle contrasts the service of sin and righteousness (6:13–23), so in the next chapter (7:4) he emphasizes the power and work of the Spirit by contrasting the service in the oldness of the letter in bondage to the law with the service in newness of the Spirit of life. In the following passages (7:14–25; 8:1–16) we see the contrast worked out; it is in light of this that the two conditions can be clearly understood. Each state has its key word, indicating the character of the life it describes. In Romans 7 we find the word *law* twenty times and the word *Spirit* only once. In the first sixteen verses of Romans 8 the word *Spirit* is seen sixteen times. The contrast is between the Christian life lived by the law and lived by the Spirit. Paul very boldly states that not only are we dead to sin and made free from sin that we might become servants of righteousness and of God (Romans 6), but also "We have been delivered from the law, having died to what we were held by, so that we should serve in the newness of the Spirit and not in the oldness of the letter" (Romans 7:6). We have here a double advance on the teaching of Romans 6. There it was the death to sin and freedom from it, here it is death to the law and freedom from it. There it was "newness of life" (6:4), as an objective reality secured to us in Christ; here it is "newness of spirit" (7:6), as a subjective experience made ours by the indwelling of the Spirit. He that would fully know and enjoy life in the Spirit must know what life in the law is and how complete is the freedom from it that the Spirit makes possible.

In the description Paul gives of the life of a believer who is still held in bondage to the law and seeks to fulfill the law there are three expressions in which the characteristic marks of that state are summed up. The first is the word *flesh*. "I am carnal [fleshly], sold under sin. In me (that is, in my flesh), nothing good dwells" (7:14, 18). If we want to understand the word *carnal,* we must refer to Paul's exposition of it in 1 Corinthians 3:1–3. He uses it there of Christians, who, though regenerate, have not yielded themselves to the Spirit entirely, so as to become spiritual. They have the Spirit, but allow the flesh to prevail. There is, therefore, a difference between Christians who are carnal or spiritual by the element that is strongest in them. As long as they have the Spirit but do not fully accept His deliverance and strive in their own strength, they do not and cannot become spiritual. Paul here describes the regenerate man. He lives in the Spirit but, according to Galatians 5:25, does not "walk in the Spirit." He has a new spirit within him, according to Ezekiel 36:26, but he has not intellectually and practically accepted God's Spirit to dwell and rule within him. He is still carnal.

The second expression we find in Romans 7:18: "To will is present with me, but how to perform what is good I do not find." In every possible variety of expression, Paul attempts to make clear the painful state of utter powerlessness in which the law and the effort to fulfill it leaves a person: "The good that I will to do, I do not do; but the evil I will not to do, that I practice" (v. 19). Willing, but not doing: such is the service of God in the oldness of the letter, in the life before Pentecost (see Matthew 26:41). The renewed spirit of the man has accepted and consented to the will of God, but the secret of the power to do, the Spirit of God as indwelling, is not yet known. In those, on the contrary, who know what life in the Spirit is, God works both to will and to do; the Christian testifies, "I can do all things through Christ who strengthens me" (Philippians

4:13). But this is only possible through faith and the Holy Spirit. As long as the believer has not consciously been made free from the law, continual failure will attend his efforts to do the will of God. He may even delight in the law of God after the inward man, but power is lacking. It is only when he submits to the law of faith—because he knows that he has been made free from the law—that he may be joined to another, to the living Jesus, working in him through His Holy Spirit so that he will indeed bring forth fruit unto God.

The third expression we must note is in verse 23 of Romans 7: "I see another law in my members, warring against the law of my mind, and bringing me into captivity to the law of sin which is in my members." This word *captivity* or *sold under sin,* suggests the idea of slaves sold into bondage without the freedom or the power to do as they wish. It points back to what he said in the beginning of the chapter: that we have been made free from the law; here is evidently one who does not yet know that freedom. And it points forward to what he says in chapter 8, verse 2: "The law of the Spirit of life in Christ Jesus has made me free from the law of sin and death." The freedom with which we have been made free in Christ, as offered according to our faith, cannot be fully accepted or experienced as long as there is a trace of a legal spirit. It is only by the Spirit of Christ within us that the full liberation is effected. As in the oldness of the letter, so in the newness of the Spirit, a two-fold relationship exists: the objective and the personal. There is the law over me and outside of me, and there is the law of sin in my members, deriving its strength from the first. Likewise, in being made free from the law, there is the objective liberty in Christ offered according to my faith. There is the subjective personal possession of that liberty, in its fullness and power, to be had alone through the Spirit dwelling and ruling in my members, even as the law of sin had done. This alone can change the cry of the captive in chapter 7, verse 24: "O wretched man that I am! Who will deliver me from this body of death?" into the song of the ransomed in v. 25: "I thank God; through Jesus Christ our Lord!" And in chapter 8, "The law of the Spirit of life in Christ Jesus has made me free from the law of sin and death" (v. 2).

How shall we regard the two conditions set before us in Romans 7:14–23 and 8:1–16? Are they interchangeable, successive, or simultaneous?

Many have thought that they are a description of the varying experiences of the believer's life. Although often by the grace of God he is able to do what is good and to live well-pleasing to God, and thus experience the grace of chapter 8, the consciousness of sin and shortcomings plunges him again into the hopelessness of chapter 7. Though sometimes the one and then the other experience may be more prominent, each day brings the experience of both.

Others have felt that this is not the life of a believer as God would have it or the life that the provision of God's grace has placed within his reach. As they saw that a life in the freedom with which Christ makes us free—when the Holy Spirit dwells within us—is within our reach, and as they entered on it, it was to them as if now and forever they had left the experience of Romans 7 far behind and they cannot but look upon it as Israel's wilderness life, a life to which they must never again return. There are many who can testify what enlightenment and blessing has come to them as they have seen what the blessed transition is from the bondage of the law to the liberty of the Spirit.

And yet however large the measure of truth to this view, it does not fully satisfy. The believer feels that there is not a day that he gets beyond the words "In me (that is, in my flesh), nothing good dwells" (7:18). Even when kept joyously in the will of God, and strengthened not only to will but also to do His will, he knows that it is not he but the grace of God. So the believer comes to see that not the two experiences, but the two conditions are simultaneous, and that even when his experience is most fully that of the law of the Spirit of life in Christ Jesus making him free, he still bears with him the body of sin and death. And so although we will always have our flesh with us as along as we live on the earth, yet the Spirit gives help and deliverance from moment to moment, and the victory can be ours if we look to Him. The "making free," which is by the Spirit, and the deliverance from the power of sin and the song of thanks to God is the continuous experience of the power of an endless life as maintained by the Spirit of Christ. As I am led of the Spirit, I am not under the law. The law's spirit of bondage, its weakness through the flesh, and the sense of condemnation and hopelessness are cast aside by the indwelling Spirit.

If there is one lesson the believer must learn who would enjoy the fullness of the Spirit, it is the one taught in chapter 8: that the law, the flesh, and self-effort are all utterly useless in enabling us to serve God. It is the Spirit within, taking the place of the law, that leads us into the liberty through which Christ has made us free. Where the Spirit of the Lord is, there is liberty.

Lord Jesus, I humbly ask you to make clear to me the secret of the life of the Spirit. Teach me what it means to become dead to the law so that my service to God is no longer in the oldness of the letter but that I am joined to another, even to yourself, the risen one, through whom we bring forth fruit unto God, serving in the newness of the Spirit.

Blessed Lord, with sorrow I confess that in my flesh nothing good dwells, that I am carnal and sold under sin. But I praise you that in answer to the cry of who will deliver me from this body of death, you have taught me to answer, "I thank God, through Jesus Christ our Lord! The law of the Spirit of life in Christ Jesus has made me free from the law of sin and death."

Teach me now to serve you in newness of life and liberty. I yield myself in full and wholehearted faith to the Holy Spirit that my life may indeed be in the glorious liberty of the children of God, in the power of an indwelling Savior, working in me both to will and to do of your good pleasure, even as the Father worked in Him. Amen.

Summary

1. It is not enough that we know that there are two masters, God and sin (Romans 6:15–22), and yield ourselves to God alone. We must see that in serving God there are two ways of doing so: the oldness of the letter (the law) and the newness of the Spirit (Romans 7:1–6). Until a soul understands the difference, confesses its danger and uselessness as illustrated in Romans 7:14–25, and utterly

forsakes it, it cannot fully know what service in newness of the Spirit is. It is only after the death of the old life and confidence in the flesh that the new life can spring up.

2. Be sure that if you ask the question "Who will deliver me from this body of death?" that you always answer it with the Scripture "I thank God; through Jesus Christ our Lord! The law of the Spirit of life in Christ Jesus has made me free." Never ask the question without giving the answer.

3. The word *law* is used in two senses. It means the inner rule, according to which all of nature acts, and is used to indicate that power, or it is used with regard to an external rule, according to which one must be taught to act who does not do so spontaneously. The external is always the proof that the inner one is lacking. When the inner law prevails, the outer is not needed. "If you are led of the Spirit, you are not under the law." The indwelling Spirit makes us free from the law.

4. The whole secret of sanctification lies in the promise of the new covenant: "I will put my law in their inward parts, and write it in their heart." Just as each plant in its growth spontaneously obeys the law put into its inmost part by God, so the believer who accepts the new covenant promise in its fullness, walks in the power of that inner law. The Spirit within frees from the law without.

Chapter 18

The Liberty
of the Spirit

*For the law of the Spirit of life in Christ Jesus has made
me free from the law of sin and death. For if you live
according to the flesh you will die; but if by the Spirit you
put to death the deeds of the body, you will live.*

Romans 8:2, 13

In the sixth chapter of Romans Paul speaks of our having
been made free from sin in Christ Jesus (vv. 18, 22). Our
death to sin in Christ has freed us from its dominion: being
made free from sin as a power, as a master, when we
accepted Christ in faith, we became servants to righteousness and to God. In the seventh chapter he speaks of our
being made free from the law (vv. 1–6). "The strength of
sin is the law" (1 Corinthians 15:56): Deliverance from sin
and the law go together. Being made free from the law, we
are united to the living Christ, that in union with Him we
might serve in newness of the Spirit (7:4–6). Paul, in these
two passages (Romans 6 and 7), presents being made free

from sin and the law, in its objective reality, as a life prepared in Christ to be accepted and maintained by faith. According to the law of a gradual growth in the Christian life, the believer must in the power of the Spirit with which he has been sealed by faith enter into this union and walk in it. As a matter of experience, almost all believers can testify that even after they have seen and accepted this teaching, their life is not what they had hoped it would be. They have found the descent into the experience of the second half of Romans 7 very real and very painful. This is because there is as a rule no other way to learn the two great lessons. The first is the uselessness of the human will, by the law urging it to obedience, ever to work out a divine righteousness in one's life. The second is the need of the conscious and full indwelling of the Holy Spirit as the only sufficient power for the life of a child of God.

In the first half of Romans 8, we have set forth this second truth. In the divine exposition of the Christian life in this epistle, and its growth in the believer, there is a distinct advance from step to step. The eighth chapter—in introducing the Holy Spirit for the first time in the unfolding of the life of faith as we have it in chapters 6–8—teaches us that it is only as the Spirit motivates our life and walk, and as He is distinctly known and accepted to do this, that we can fully possess and enjoy the riches of grace that are ours in Christ. Let everyone who would know what it is to be dead to sin and alive to God, to be free from sin and the law and joined to Him who was raised from the dead, come to find the strength he needs in that Spirit through whom union with Christ can be maintained as a divine experience and His life be lived within us in power and truth.

Of the first half of the eighth chapter, the second verse is the center. It reveals the wonderful secret of how our freedom from sin and the law may become a living and abiding experience. A believer may know that he is free and yet have to admit that his experience is that of a hopeless captive. The freedom is so entirely *in* Christ Jesus, and the maintenance of the living union with Him so distinctly and entirely a work of divine power, that it is only as we see that the divine Spirit dwells within us for this very purpose, and know how to accept and yield to His working it, that we can truly stand perfect and complete in the liberty with which Christ has made us free. The life and the liberty of Romans 6 and 7:1–6 are only fully ours as we can say, "The law of the Spirit of life in Christ Jesus has made me free from the law of sin and death" (8:2). Through the whole Christian life this principle rules: "According to your faith let it be to you" (Matthew 9:29). As the Holy Spirit, the Spirit of faith, reveals the greatness of God's resurrection power working in us, and as faith in the indwelling Spirit yields to receive that power to the fullest, all that is available to us in Christ Jesus becomes manifest in our daily personal experience. When we perceive the difference between this and the previous teaching (Romans 6–7:6), and when we see what a distinct advantage there is in it, the unique and most glorious place that the Holy Spirit as God holds in the plan of redemption and the life of faith will open up to us. We learn with this that as divinely perfect as the life of liberty in Christ Jesus is, so also does the power of that life enable us to walk in the freedom of the Holy Spirit. The living assurance and experience of the Holy Spirit's indwelling will become to us the first necessity of the new life, inseparable from the person and presence of Jesus Christ our Lord.

Again, "The law of the Spirit of life in Christ Jesus has made us free from the law of sin and death." Paul here contrasts the two opposing laws: the one of sin and death in the members, the other of the Spirit of life ruling and quickening even the mortal body. Under the former we see the believer sighing as a hopeless captive. In the second half of Romans 6, Paul addresses him as made free from sin and by voluntary surrender become a servant to God and to righteousness. He has forsaken the service of sin and yet it often masters him. The promise "Sin shall not"—never for a moment—"have dominion over you" (6:14) has not been realized. To will is present, but how to perform he knows not. "O wretched man that I am! Who will deliver me from this body of death?" (7:24) is the cry of futility amid all his efforts to keep the law. "I thank God; through Jesus Christ our Lord!" (7:25) is the answer of faith that claims the deliverance in Christ from this power that has held him captive. From the law—the dominion of sin and death in the members—and its actual power in motivating sin, there is deliverance. That deliverance is a new law, a mighty force, an actual power making free from sin. As real as was the energy of sin working in our members is the energy of the Spirit dwelling in our bodies. It is the Spirit of life that is in Christ. Out of that life, when filled as it was in the resurrection and ascension with the mighty energy of God's power (Ephesians 1:17, 21), and admitted on the throne to the omnipotence of God as the eternal Spirit—out of that life there descended the Holy Spirit, himself God. The law, the power, the dominion of the life in Christ Jesus made me free from the law, the dominion of sin and death in my members, with a freedom as real as was the slavery. From the very first beginnings of the new life, it was the Spirit who breathed faith in Christ. When we first entered into justification, it was He who shed abroad the love of God in our hearts. It was He who led us to see Christ as our life as well as our righteousness. But all of this was in most cases still accompanied by a lack of knowledge of His presence and of the great need for a supply of His almighty power. As the believer in Romans 7:14–23 is brought to the discovery of the deep-rooted legality of the old nature and its absolute impotence, the truth of the Holy Spirit and of the mighty power with which He does, in a practical sense, make us free from the power of sin and death is understood as never before. Our text becomes a declaration of the highest faith and experience combined: "The law of the Spirit of life in Christ Jesus has made me free from the law of sin and death." As real, mighty, and spontaneous as the law of sin in the members was, so likewise is the law of the Spirit of life in those members.

The believer who wants to live fully in this liberty of life in Christ Jesus will easily understand what the path is in which he will learn to walk. The message of Romans 8 is the goal to which Romans 6 and 7 lead. In faith, he will first have to study and accept all that is taught in these two earlier chapters of his being in Christ Jesus, dead to sin and alive to God, free from sin and the law and joined to Christ. "If you abide in My word, you are My disciples indeed. And you shall know the truth, and the truth shall make you free" (John 8:31–32). Let the Word of God, as it teaches you of your union with Christ, be the life-soil in which your faith and life daily takes root; abide, dwell in it, and let it abide in you. To meditate, hold fast, hide in the heart the word of this gospel, to assimilate it by faith, is the way to grasp the truth the Scripture teaches. If your passage through the experience of carnality and captivity to which the attempts to fulfill the law bring us appears to be anything but progress, remember that it is in the utter despair of self that entire surrender to the Spirit is born and strengthened. Ceasing from all hope through the flesh and the law is entrance into the liberty of the Spirit.

To walk in the paths of this new life it will be particularly good to remember what is meant by the expression "walk according to the Spirit." The Spirit is to lead, to reveal the path. This implies surrender, obedience, waiting to be guided. He is to be the ruling power; we are in all things to live and act under the law and the authority of the Spirit. A holy fear of grieving Him, watchfulness to know His leading, daily faith in His presence, humble adoration of Him as God—all must mark such a life. The words Paul uses toward the close of this section are to express our goal: "If by the Spirit you put to death the deeds of the body, you will live" (Romans 8:13). The Holy Spirit possessing, inspiring, and motivating all the powers of our spirit and soul, entering into us and enabling us to die to the deeds of the body, is what we may count upon. This is the sanctification of the Spirit to which we have been called.

We walk by faith and not by sight: this is what we particularly need to remember in regard to our walking according to the Spirit. Because the visible manifestation of Christ and His work is so much more intelligible than the revelation of the Spirit's work in us, seeking the leading of the Spirit generally calls for more faith. The power of the Spirit hides himself away in union with our weakness to undertake for us in our daily living. It takes patient perseverance to come into the full consciousness of His indwelling presence.

We need the direct, fresh anointing day by day from the Holy One, in fellowship with Christ. If ever the word "Only believe!" is needed, it is now. Believe in the Father's promise. Believe in the Son and His life that is yours by His Spirit. Believe in the Holy Spirit as the bearer, communicator, and maintainer of the life and presence of Jesus with you. Believe in Him as *within* you.

Ever blessed God and Father, we do praise you for the wonderful gift of your Holy Spirit, in whom you together with your Son come to make your home in us. We bless you for the wonderful gift of eternal life that your beloved Son bought us. And we thank you that the law of the Spirit of life in Christ Jesus makes us free from the law of sin and death.

Our Father, we pray that you would reveal to us in full and blessed experience what the perfect law of liberty is, that it is the power of a continuous and unfading existence, none other than eternal life. It is the law of the Spirit of life in Christ Jesus, the Holy Spirit revealing and glorifying Christ in us as an indwelling presence. O Father, open our eyes and strengthen our faith that we may believe that the law of the Spirit is indeed greater than the law of sin in our members. Teach this to all your dear children. Amen.

Summary

1. Ask if this is your experience: Are you living in the liberty of the law of the Spirit of life in Christ Jesus? Are

you truly delivered from the law of sin and death in your members?

2. Let us remember the path as set before us in the gospel of Christ by Paul. You were reconciled to God by the death of His Son; you are now to be saved by His life (Romans 5:10). By faith you know that that life is yours in all its power (6:11). In the strength of it you gave yourself to be a servant of God (6:15–22). But the service was not to be in a legal sense under the law, but in the newness of the Spirit (7:1–6). Because you did not understand this, you sought in the power of the new life to fulfill the law you delighted in, and yet utterly failed (7:14, 25). This is where the Holy Spirit comes in (8:1–16). Faith in Jesus and His life leads the way to the life of the Spirit in you. The Holy Spirit frees from the law, and maintains the life of Christ in the power of His living presence. The message of Romans 8:2 is the key to the blessed life.

3. As Adam's life is reproduced in the entire human family, so the *new life* of the God-man flows to all His people. Our life is the reproduction of Christ's spiritual life. The new birth connects us with the second man, Jesus Christ.

4. Would you live that life? Remember our lesson: Acknowledge the Holy Spirit dwelling in you. Study, above all, to be full of faith in His presence as the revealer of Christ and His life in you. Surrender to Him to rule, be ready to wait on Him and to walk after Him. The law of the Spirit, the force or power of an inward life, the law of the Spirit of life in Christ Jesus has made us free from the law of sin and death.

Chapter 19

The Leading
of the Spirit

*For as many as are led by the Spirit of God,
these are sons of God.*

Romans 8:14

To many Christians, the leading of the Spirit is thought of
as a pleasant way to speak of guidance for the Christian life.
When it comes to some opinion or obligation, the answer
to a problem or the distinct direction in the performance
of some Christian work, most would be glad for some indication from the Spirit as to the right choice. But they long
and ask for it in vain. When at times they think they have
it, it does not bring the assurance, the comfort, or the success that they think ought to be the sign that something is
truly of the Spirit. And so the precious truth of the Spirit's
leading, instead of being an end to all controversy and the
solution for every difficulty, or simply a source of strength,
becomes a cause for perplexity and great difficulty.

The error comes from not accepting the truth that we

have spoken of: that the teaching and the leading of the Spirit is first given in the life, not in the mind. The life is stirred and strengthened; the life becomes the light. As conformity to this world and its spirit is crucified and dies, and as we deliberately deny the will of the flesh, we are renewed in the spirit of our mind, and so the mind becomes able to prove and know the good and perfect and acceptable will of God (Romans 12:2).

This connection between the practical, sanctifying work of the Spirit in our inner life and His leading comes out very clearly in our context. "If by the Spirit you put to death the deeds of the body, you will live" (8:13). Then immediately follows, "For as many as are led by the Spirit of God, these are sons of God" (v. 14). That is, as many as allow themselves to be led by Him in putting to death the deeds of the body, these are sons of God. The Holy Spirit is the Spirit of the life of Christ Jesus, who works in us as a divine life-power. He is the Spirit of holiness, and only in holiness will He lead. Through Him God works in us both to will and to do of His good pleasure; through Him God makes us perfect in every good work to do His will, working in us that which is well-pleasing in His sight. To be led of the Spirit implies in the first place the surrender to His work as He convinces of sin and cleanses soul and body for His temple. It is as the indwelling Spirit, filling, sanctifying, and ruling the heart and life that He enlightens and leads.

In this book there is no separate chapter on the sanctification of the Spirit, or on Him as the Spirit of holiness. The reason is that this work is a continuation of a previous volume, *Holy in Christ* (retitled *The Path to Holiness*, 2001, Bethany House), in which there was occasion to speak of what is meant by holiness both as the attribute and the work of the Holy Spirit.

In the study of what the leading of the Spirit means, it is of primary importance to grasp this thought in all its significance. Only the spiritual mind can discern spiritual things and receive the leading of the Spirit. The mind must first become spiritual to become capable of spiritual guidance. Paul said to the Corinthians that because, though born again, they were still carnal—babes in Christ—he had not been able to teach them spiritual truth. If this is true of the teaching that comes through men, how much more is it true of the direct teaching of the Spirit, by which He leads into all truth. The deepest mysteries of Scripture, as far as they are apprehended by human thought, can be studied and accepted and even taught by the unsanctified mind. But the leading of the Spirit—we cannot repeat it too often—does not begin in the region of thought or feeling (the soul). Deeper down, in the hidden life of the spirit of man, from which issues the power that molds the will and fashions the character, there the Holy Spirit takes up residence, breathes, moves, and impels.

He leads by inspiring us with a life and disposition out of which right purposes and decisions come. "That you may be filled with the knowledge of His will in all wisdom and spiritual understanding" (Colossians 1:9): Paul's prayer teaches us that it is only to a spiritual understanding that the knowledge of God's will can be given. And spiritual understanding comes with the growth of the spiritual man and faithfulness to the spiritual life. He that would have the leading of the Spirit must yield himself to have his life filled with the Spirit. It was when Christ was baptized with the

Spirit that "being filled with the Holy Spirit . . . [he] was led by the Spirit into the wilderness" (Luke 4:1), and that he "returned in the power of the Spirit to Galilee" (v. 14) and began His ministry in Nazareth with the words, "The Spirit of the Lord is upon Me" (v. 18).

It is not hard to understand that to enjoy the leading of the Spirit requires a teachable servant's mind. The Spirit is not only hindered by the flesh as the power that commits sin, but even more by the flesh as the power that seeks to serve God. To be able to discern the Spirit's teaching, Scripture tells us that the ear must be circumcised—in a circumcision not made with hands—in the putting off of the body of the flesh, in the circumcision of Christ. The will and wisdom of the flesh must be feared, denied, put to death. The ear must be closed to all that the flesh and its wisdom, whether in the self or in others, would say. In all our thoughts of God or study of His Word, in all our efforts toward worship and service for Him, there must be a continued distrust and putting away of self and a patient waiting on God by the Holy Spirit to teach and lead us. The soul that daily, hourly waits for divine leading, for the light of knowledge and of calling, will surely receive it. If you would be led of the Spirit, give up, day by day, your own will and wisdom, your whole life and being to God and His work. The fire will descend and consume the sacrifice.

The leading of the Spirit comes in response to faith—in two senses. The leading will begin when we learn to cultivate and act upon the confidence that the Holy Spirit is *in us* and He is doing His work. The Spirit's full indwelling is the crowning act of God's redemptive work. Here, if anywhere, faith is needed. Faith is the faculty of the soul that recognizes the unseen, the divine; it receives the impression of the divine presence when God draws near and accepts what He brings and gives. In the Holy Spirit is the most intimate communication of the divine life; here faith may not judge by what it feels or understands, but submits to God and allows Him to do what He has promised. It meditates and worships, it prays and trusts, it yields the whole soul in adoring acceptance and thanksgiving to the Savior's word "He will be in you." It rejoices in the assurance that the Holy Spirit, the mighty power of God, dwells within us in His own way; faith may depend upon it.

Beyond a general faith in the indwelling of the Spirit, faith is also exercised in regard to each part of the leading. When there is a question I have put before the Lord, and my soul has in quiet expectancy waited for Him to answer, I must in faith trust God that His guidance will not be withheld. As we have said before, we cannot expect the everyday leading of the Spirit in sudden impulses or strong impressions, or in heavenly voices and remarkable interpositions. There are souls to whom such leading undoubtedly is given, and the time may come when our thoughts and feelings may become the conscious vehicles of His voice. But this and the growth of our spiritual capacity we must leave to Him. The lower steps of the ladder are low enough for the weakest to reach; God intends that every child of His be led by the Spirit every day. Begin following the Spirit's leading by believing not only that the Spirit is within you but that He also now undertakes the work for which you ask and trust Him. Yield yourself to God in undivided surrender. Believe with implicit confidence that God's acceptance of the surrender means that you are under the control of the Spirit. Through Him Jesus guides, rules, and sanctifies you.

But are we not in danger of being led away by the imaginings of our own hearts and counting as leading of the Spirit what really is a delusion of the flesh? And if so, where is our safeguard against such error? Ordinarily the answer given to this last question is the Word of God. And yet that answer is only half the truth. Far too many have used the Word of God to oppose the danger of fanaticism, but interpreted by human reason or by the church have erred no less than those they oppose. The real answer is: The Word of God as *taught by the Spirit of God.* It is in the perfect harmony of the two that safety is found. Let us on the one hand remember that as the Word of God was given by the Spirit of God, so each word must be interpreted to us by that same Spirit. That this interpretation comes alone from the indwelling Spirit we need hardly repeat; it is only the spiritual man, whose inner life is under the control of the Spirit, who can discern the spiritual meaning of the Word. Let us on the other hand hold on to the fact that as all the Word is given by the Spirit, so His great work is to honor that Word and to unfold the fullness of divine truth treasured there. Our assurance of safety in the path of the Spirit's guidance is not in the Spirit without the Word, and not in the Word without the Spirit, but in the Word and the Spirit both dwelling richly within us and our being committed to implicit obedience.

This brings us back to the lesson we stressed at the beginning: the leading of the Spirit cannot be separated from the sanctifying of the Spirit. Let each one who would be led of the Spirit begin by giving himself to be led of the

Word as far as he knows it. Begin at the beginning: Obey the commandments. Jesus said he that will do, shall know. Keep the commandments, and the Father will send the Spirit. Give up every sin. Yield in everything to the voice of conscience. Commit yourself to God and let Him have His way. Through the Spirit, put to death the deeds of the flesh. As a son of God place yourself at the entire disposal of the Spirit, to follow where He leads. And the Spirit himself, this same Spirit through whom you put away all sin and yield yourself to be led as a son, will bear witness with your spirit—in a joy and power until now unknown—that you are indeed a child of God, enjoying all the privileges of the child of a King.

Dear Father, I thank you for the message that as many as are led by the Spirit of God are the children of God. You would not have your children guided by anyone less than your own Holy Spirit. As He dwelt in your Son, and led Him, so He leads us, with a divine and blessed leading.

Father, you know how by reason of our not fully knowing and not perfectly following this holy guidance, we are often unable to know His voice, and the thought of the leading of the Spirit is more a burden than a joy. Father, forgive us. Be pleased to quicken our faith in the simplicity and certainty of the leading of the Spirit so that with our whole heart we may yield ourselves from now on to walk in it.

Father, here I do yield myself to you as your child, in everything to be led by your Spirit. My own wisdom, my own will, my own way, I forsake. Daily would I wait in dependence upon your guidance. May my spirit ever be quieted in your holy presence, while I wait to let Him rule within. As I through the Spirit die to the deeds of the body, may I be trans-formed by the renewing of my mind to know your good and perfect will. May my whole being be so completely under the rule of the indwelling, sanctifying Spirit that the spiritual understanding of your will may be the rule of my life. Amen.

Summary

1. Note carefully the order of the three verses: 8:13–15. Putting to death the deeds of the body through the indwelling Spirit precedes the leading of the Spirit. And these two prepare the way for the abiding witness to our sonship.

2. One of the deepest teachings of the Word in regard to sanctification is our putting to death the deeds of the flesh. The *temptation* to sin remains to the end. But the deeds of the body, each sin as it presents itself, can be denied. It is the presence and life of Christ, through the Holy Spirit, that makes this possible. The believer who yields to Him can do this through the Spirit. Sin can be put to death. To do this we must be full of the Spirit of life in Christ Jesus.

3. The putting to death of sin has a threefold reference. When a believer has fallen into sin, but repents of it, the Spirit, by the application of the blood, nullifies it. When one fears the evil tendency that may return and betray him, the Holy Spirit is able to keep that one from sin by the power of Christ's death. But let us remember, it is by revealing Jesus in the power of His death and life, and filling the soul with Him, that the deeds of the body can be put to death through the Spirit. The Spirit enables us to do what is necessary.

4. There can be no guidance that is perpetual. The advantage of a year may be lost in an hour. If we act independently of the Spirit in little things, we shall look for Him in vain in the great things.

Chapter 20

The Spirit of Prayer

Now He who searches the hearts knows what the mind of the Spirit is, because He makes intercession for the saints according to the will of God. And we know that all things work together for good to those who love God, to those who are the called according to His purpose.

Romans 8:26–27

Of the offices of the Holy Spirit, the one that leads us most deeply into the understanding of His place in the divine economy of grace and into the mystery of the Holy Trinity is the work He does as the Spirit of prayer. We have the Father *to* whom we pray and who hears prayer. We have the Son *through* whom we pray and through whom we receive and appropriate the answer because of our union with Him. And we have the Holy Spirit *by* whom we pray, who prays in us, according to the will of God, with such deep, unutterable sounds that God searches our hearts to know the mind of the Spirit. Just as wonderful and real as the divine work of God on the throne, graciously hearing our prayers, so is the work of the Son securing and transmitting the answer from above, and the work of the Holy Spirit in us, interceding on our behalf. The intercession within is as divine as the intercession above. Let us look at why this is so and what it teaches.

In the creation of the world we see how it was the work of the Spirit to put himself into contact with the dark and lifeless matter of chaos and by His quickening energy to impart to it the power of life and fruitfulness. It was only after it had been thus vitalized by Him that the Word of God gave it form and called forth the various kinds of life and beauty we now enjoy. Likewise, in the creation of man it was the Spirit that was breathed into the body that had been formed from the ground and that united itself with what would otherwise be dead matter. Even so in the person of Jesus, a body was prepared for Him through the work of the Spirit. Through the Spirit His body was quickened from the grave, and it is through the Spirit that our bodies are made the temples of God—the very members of our body the members of Christ. We think of the Spirit in connection with the spiritual nature of the divine being, far removed from the vileness and frailty of physical substance. But it is the work of the Spirit to unite himself particularly with what is material, to lift it up into His own Spirit-nature, and so create the highest form of perfection—a spiritual body.

This view of the Spirit's work is essential to the understanding of the place He takes in the divine work of redemption. In each part of that work there is a special office assigned to each of the three persons of the Trinity. The Father is the unseen God, the Author of all. The Son of God is the form of God revealed, made manifest, and brought near to us. The Spirit of God is the power of God dwelling in His people and working in them what the Father and the Son desire for us. Not only in the individual, but in the church as a whole, what the Father has purposed, and the Son has procured, can be appropriated and made effectual in the body of Christ only through the continual intervention and active operation of the Holy Spirit.

This is especially true of intercessory prayer. The coming of the kingdom of God, the increase of grace, knowledge, and holiness in believers, their growing devotion to God's work, the effectual working of God's power on the unconverted through the means of grace—all of this awaits us from God through Christ. But it cannot come unless it is desired and sought, expected, believed, and hoped for. This is now the wonderful position the Holy Spirit occupies—He has been assigned the task of preparing the body of Christ to reach out, receive, and secure what has been provided in the fullness of Christ, our Head. For the communication of the Father's love and blessing, both the Son and the Spirit must work. The Son receives from the Father, reveals it and brings it near; the Spirit from within awakens the soul to meet its Lord. As indispensable as the unceasing work of Christ, asking and receiving from the Father, is the unceasing intercession of the Spirit.

The light that is cast upon this holy mystery by the words of our text is awesome. In the life of faith and prayer there are operations of the Spirit in which the Word of God is made clear to our understanding, and our faith knows how to express what it needs and asks. But there are also operations of the Spirit, deeper than thoughts or feelings, where He works desires and yearnings into our spirit, in the secret springs of life, which only God can discover and understand. In our spirits is the thirst for God himself, the living God. There is the longing "to know the love of Christ which passes knowledge" and to "be filled with all the fullness of God," the hope in Him "who is able to do exceedingly abundantly above all that we ask or think" (Ephesians 3:19–20) even what has not "entered into the heart of man" (1 Corinthians 2:9). When these aspirations take possession of us, we begin to pray for what cannot be expressed, and our only comfort is that the Spirit prays with unutterable yearnings in a language He alone knows and understands.

To the Corinthians, Paul says, "I will pray with the spirit, and I will also pray with the understanding" (1 Corinthians 14:15). Under the influence of the moving of the Holy Spirit and His miraculous gifts, the danger was to neglect the understanding. The danger in these latter days is the opposite: to pray with understanding is universal. We need to be reminded that with the prayer of understanding there must be prayer in the Spirit (Jude 20; Ephesians 6:18). We need to give due place to each of the twofold operations of the Spirit. God's Word must dwell in us richly, our faith must hold it clearly and intelligently, and we must plead it in prayer. To have the words of Christ abiding in us, filling our life and conduct, is one of the secrets of effectual prayer. And yet we must remember, too, that in the inner sanctuary of our being, in the area of the unutterable and inconceivable, the Spirit prays for us what we do not know and cannot express (1 Corinthians 2:6–11). As we grow in the apprehension of the divinity of the Holy Spirit and the reality of His indwelling, we shall recognize how infinitely beyond our mind's grasp is the divine hunger with which

He draws us heavenward. We shall feel the need of cultivating the activity of faith that seeks to grasp and obey God's Word and from that learn to pray. As we pray we will remember how infinitely above our apprehension is God and the spirit-world that we enter through prayer. Let us believe and rejoice that where heart and flesh fail, God is our strength; His Holy Spirit within the innermost sanctuary of our spirit does His unceasing work of intercession and prays within us according to God's will. As we pray, let us worship in holy stillness, and yield ourselves to that blessed Paraclete, who alone truly is the Spirit of supplication.

"We know not what we should pray for as we ought," but "He makes intercession for the saints" (Romans 8:26–27). It is particularly in intercessory prayer that we may count upon the deep, unutterable, but all-prevailing intercession of the Spirit.

What a privilege to be the temple from which the Holy Spirit cries to the Father His unceasing "Abba" and offers His prayers too deep for words. What an awesome thought it is that the eternal Son dwelt in the flesh in Jesus of Nazareth and prayed to the Father as a man, and then to know that the eternal Spirit dwells in us—sinful flesh that we are—and speaks to the Father through us even as the Son did. Who would not yield himself to this blessed Spirit to be made fit to share in the mighty intercessory work through which alone the kingdom of God can be revealed? The path is open and invites us all. Let the Holy Spirit have full control of your life. Believe in the possibility of His making your personality and consciousness the place of His indwelling. Believe in the certainty of His working and praying through you in a way that no human mind can comprehend. Believe that in the secret, quiet, steadiness of that work, His almighty power is perfecting the divine purpose of your blessed Lord. Live as one in whom that which passes understanding has become truth and life, in whom the intercession of the Spirit is part of daily life.

Most Holy God, once more I bow in adoration in your presence to thank you for the precious privilege of prayer. I thank you for the grace that has given us your Son, our intercessor above, and your Spirit, our intercessor within.

You know, Father, how I can scarcely take in the thought that your Holy Spirit dwells in me and prays through my frail prayers. Reveal to me all that hinders His taking full possession of me and filling me with the consciousness of His presence. Allow my inmost being and my outward life to be so under His leading that I may have the spiritual understanding that knows how to ask according to your will as well as the living faith that receives what it asks. When I know not what or how to pray, O Father, teach me to bow in silent worship and wait before you, knowing that He breathes the wordless prayer that you alone understand.

As a temple of your Holy Spirit, I yield myself to be used in His work of intercession. May my whole heart be filled with longing for Christ's honor and His love for the lost. My heart's cry is for the coming of your kingdom. Amen.

Summary

1. Reading about the Holy Spirit's place in intercessory prayer, we can better understand our Lord's prayers on his last night on earth with their oft-repeated "Not as I

will, but as You will" and "Your will be done" (Matthew 26). He intends that we have the Holy Spirit praying in us and through us, guiding our desires and strengthening our faith. He expects us to give our whole being to the indwelling of the Spirit that He might freely pray through us according to God's will.

2. "We do not know what we should pray for as we ought" (Romans 8:26): How often this has been a burden, a sorrow! Let it from now on be a comfort. Because we do not know, we may stand aside and give place to the One who does know. We can believe that in our stammering, in our sighs, the intercessor is pleading for us. Let us not fear to believe that in our ignorance and weakness the Holy Spirit is doing His work.

3. The great *ought* of prayer is faith. The Spirit is the Spirit of faith, deeper than thought. Be of good courage, our faith is being kept by the Spirit.

4. Here, as elsewhere, all leads to one point: The Holy Spirit's indwelling must be our goal. In faith that holds the promise, in watchfulness that waits for and follows His leading, in the entire surrender of the self to death, that He alone may rule and reign, let us yield to our God to be filled with His Spirit.

Chapter 21

The Holy Spirit
and Conscience

*I tell the truth in Christ, I am not lying, my conscience
also bearing me witness in the Holy Spirit.*

Romans 9:1

*The Spirit Himself bears witness with our spirit
that we are children of God.*

Romans 8:16

God's highest glory is His holiness by virtue of which He
hates and destroys evil, loves and works good. In humankind, the conscience has the same task. It condemns sin and
approves what is right and good. Conscience is the remnant
of God's image, the nearest approach to the divine, the
guardian of God's honor amid the ruin of the fall. God's
work of redemption begins with the conscience. The Spirit
of God is the Spirit of holiness; conscience is a spark of
divine holiness. Harmony between the work of the Holy
Spirit in renewing and sanctifying man and the work of

conscience is intimate, essential. The believer who would be filled with the Holy Spirit and experience to the fullest the blessings He gives must first see that he yields to his conscience the place and honor it is due. Faithfulness to conscience is the first step in the path of restoration to the holiness of God. Conscientiousness is the groundwork and characteristic of true spirituality. As the conscience witnesses to a ready response toward God, and as the Spirit witnesses to God's acceptance of our faith and obedience, so the two in time become one.

Conscience can be compared to the window of a room through which the light of heaven shines and through which we can see heaven. The heart is the chamber in which our life dwells, our ego, or soul, with its powers and affections. On the walls of that chamber is written the law of God. Even in heathen peoples it is still partly legible, though sadly darkened and defaced. In the believer the law is written anew by the Holy Spirit in letters of light, which are often dim at first, but grow clearer and brighter as they are exposed to the light coming from without. With every sin I commit, the light that shines in makes it manifest and condemns it. If the sin is not confessed and forsaken, the stain remains, and conscience becomes defiled because the mind refuses the teaching of the light (Titus 1:15). And so with sin upon sin the window gets darker and darker, until the light can barely shine through at all and the Christian can sin undisturbed—the conscience to a large extent blinded and without feeling. In His work of renewal the Holy Spirit does not create new faculties: He renews and sanctifies those already in existence. Conscience is the work of the Spirit of God, the Creator. As the Spirit of God, the

Redeemer, His first care is to restore what sin has defiled. It is only by restoring conscience to its full and healthy function and revealing in it the wonderful grace of Christ, "the Spirit bearing witness with our spirit," that He enables the believer to live a life in the full light of God's favor. It is as the window of the heart that looks heavenward is cleansed and kept clean that we can walk in the light.

The work of the Spirit on the conscience is threefold. Through conscience the Spirit causes *the light of God's holy law* to shine into the heart. A room may have the curtains drawn, even shutters closed: This does not prevent the lightning flash from time to time to shine into the darkness. Conscience may be so sin-stained and seared that the strong man within dwells in peace. When the lightning from Sinai flashes into the heart, conscience awakens and is ready to admit and sustain the condemnation. Both the law and the gospel, with their call to repentance and their conviction of sin, appeal to the conscience. And it is not until conscience has agreed to the charge of transgression and unbelief that deliverance can truly come.

It is through the conscience that the Spirit likewise causes *the light of mercy* to shine. When the windows of a house are stained, they can be washed. "How much more shall the blood of Christ, who through the eternal Spirit offered Himself without spot to God, cleanse your conscience from dead works to serve the living God?" (Hebrews 9:14; 10:2, 22). The aim of the blood of Christ is to reach the conscience, to silence its accusations, and cleanse it, until it can testify: Every stain is removed; the love of the Father allows Christ, in unclouded brightness, into my soul. This is the privilege of every believer. It becomes certain when the conscience says Amen to God's message of the power of Jesus' blood.

The conscience that has been cleansed in the blood must be kept clean by a walk in obedience of faith with the light of God's favor shining on it. To the promise of the indwelling Spirit and His undertaking to lead in all of God's will, conscience must agree and testify that He has done the work. The believer is called to walk in humility and watchfulness, lest in anything his conscience should accuse him of not having done what he knew to be right or having done what was not of faith. He may be content with nothing less than Paul's testimony: "For our boasting is this: the testimony of our conscience that we conducted ourselves in the world in simplicity and godly sincerity, not with fleshly wisdom but by the grace of God" (2 Corinthians 1:12). (Compare Acts 23:1; 24:16; 2 Timothy 1:3.) Note these words well: "Our boasting is this: the testimony of our conscience." It is as the window is kept clean and bright by our abiding in the light that we can have fellowship with the Father and the Son. The love of heaven shines in unclouded, and our love responds in childlike trust. "Beloved, if our heart does not condemn us, we have confidence toward God ... because we keep His commandments and do those things that are pleasing in His sight" (1 John 3:21–22).

The maintenance of a good conscience toward God is essential to the life of faith. The believer must be satisfied with nothing less than this. He may be assured that it is within his reach. The believers in the Old Testament by faith had the witness that they pleased God (Hebrews 11:4–6, 39). In the New Testament it is set before us not only as a command to be obeyed but also as a grace wrought by God himself. "That you may walk worthy of the Lord, fully pleasing Him, being fruitful in every good work, and increasing in the knowledge of God; strengthened with all might, according to His glorious power. . . . That our God would . . . fulfill all the good pleasure of His goodness and the work of faith with power. Working in you what is well pleasing in His sight" (Colossians 1:10–11; 2 Thessalonians 1:11; Hebrews 13:21). The more we seek this testimony of conscience—that we are doing what is well pleasing to God—the more we will feel the liberty with every failure that overtakes us to look immediately to the blood of Christ. The blood that cleanses the conscience acts in the power of eternal life that knows no intermission or change and that saves completely. "If we walk in the light, as He is in the light, we have fellowship one with another, and the blood of Jesus Christ cleanses us from all sin" (1 John 1:7).

The cause of the weakness of our faith is lack of a clean conscience. Notice how closely Paul connects them in 1 Timothy: "Love from a pure heart, from a *good conscience,* and from sincere *faith*" (1:5). "Having *faith* and a *good conscience,* which some having rejected, concerning the faith have suffered shipwreck" (1:19). And especially (3:9), "Holding the mystery of *the faith* with a *pure conscience*" (emphasis added). The conscience is the seat of faith. He that would grow strong in faith and have confidence toward God must know that he is pleasing Him (1 John 3:21- 22). Jesus said clearly that it is for those who love Him and keep His commandments that the promise of the Spirit is intended. How can we confidently claim these promises unless in childlike simplicity our conscience can testify that we fulfill the conditions? Until the church can rise to the height of her holy calling as intercessor, and claim these unlimited promises as within her reach, believers will draw nigh to their Father, boasting, like Paul, in the testimony of their conscience—that by the grace of God they are walking in holiness and godly sincerity. We must realize that this is the deepest humility and brings the most glory to God's offer of grace—giving up our ideas of what we can attain and accepting God's declaration of what He desires and promises as the standard of what we are to be.

How is this blessed life to be attained in which we can daily appeal to God and men with Paul: "I tell the truth in Christ . . . my conscience also bearing me witness in the Holy Spirit"? The first step is to humble yourself under the reproof of conscience. Don't be content with a general confession that there is something wrong. Beware of confusing actual transgression with temptation to sin. If we are to die to sin by the indwelling Spirit, we must first deal with the practice of sin. Allow conscience time in silent submission and humiliation to reprove and condemn any sin. Tell your Father that you are, by His grace, going to obey—even in the smallest thing. Accept anew Christ's offer to take entire possession of your heart, to dwell in you as Lord and keeper. Trust Him by His Holy Spirit to do this even when you feel weak and helpless. Remember that obedience, the taking and keeping of Christ's words in your will and life, is the only way to prove the reality of your surrender to Him or your interest in His work and grace. Vow in faith that by God's grace you will seek to *always* have a conscience void of offense toward God and others.

When you have taken these steps, you are being faithful

in keeping your conscience pure, and the light will shine more brightly from heaven into your heart, revealing sin and emphasizing the law written there by the Spirit. Be willing to be taught; trust that the Spirit will teach you. Every honest effort to keep the blood-cleansed conscience clean, in the light of God, will be met with the aid of the Spirit. Yield yourself wholeheartedly to God's will and to the power of His Holy Spirit.

As you bow to the reproofs of conscience and give yourself wholly to do God's will, your courage will grow strong that it is possible to have a conscience void of offense. The witness of conscience as to what you are doing and will do by grace will be met by the witness of the Spirit as to what Christ is doing and will do. In childlike simplicity you will seek to begin each day with the simple prayer: Father, there is nothing now between you and your child. My conscience, divinely cleansed in the blood, bears witness. Let not even the shadow of a cloud intervene this day. In everything I would do your will: Your Spirit dwells in me, and leads me, and makes me strong in Christ. You will enter upon that life that rejoices in free grace alone when it says at the close of each day, Our boasting is this: the testimony of our conscience, that in holiness and godly sincerity, by the grace of God, we have conducted ourselves in the world.

Gracious God, I thank you for the voice you have given in our hearts to testify whether or not we are pleasing to you. I thank you that when that witness condemned me, with its agreement to the condemnation of your law, you gave the blood of your Son to cleanse. I thank you that at this moment my conscience can say Amen to the voice of the blood and that I can look up to you in full assurance and a heart cleansed from an evil conscience.

I thank you for the witness from heaven to what Jesus has done and is doing for me and in me. I thank you that He glorifies Christ in me, gives me His presence and His power, and transforms me into His likeness. I thank you that the presence and the work of your Spirit in my heart and my conscience can likewise say Amen.

I desire this day to walk before you with a clear conscience, to do nothing that might grieve you or the Lord Jesus. I ask you that in the power of the Holy Spirit, the cleansing in the blood might be a living, continual, and effectual deliverance from the power of sin, binding and strengthening me to your perfect service. And may my whole walk with you be in the joy of the united witness of conscience and your Spirit that I am well pleasing to you. Amen.

Summary

1. In a well-ordered house the windows are kept clean, especially where the owner loves to rest and look out on some beautiful view. See to it every day that the windows of your soul are kept clean so that not a shadow of cloud obstructs the light from above. Involuntary sin is at once cleansed by the blood if faith claims it. Let every failure be at once confessed and cleansed. Be content with nothing less than walking in the light of His countenance every day.

2. When we are faithful over a few things, God will give us more responsibility. Faithfulness to conscience as the lesser light is the only way to the enjoyment of the Spirit

as the greater light. If we are unfaithful to the witness we have, how can God commit to us the true witness? We cannot repeat it too often: A tender conscience is the only way to true spirituality.

3. Is not the preaching of conscience and to conscience in connection with the preaching of the blood what is needed in the church? Some preach conscience and say little of the blood. Some preach the blood and say little of conscience. This is one of God's wonderful words, "How much more shall the blood of Christ ... cleanse your conscience from dead works to serve the living God?" (Hebrews 9:14). Conscience is the power that pleads for responsibility and doing what is right. And the object and effect of the blood, when preached and believed as God would have it, is to restore conscience to its full power. The power of holiness lies in the careful maintenance of the conscience and the wonderful harmony of the conscience with the blood of Christ.

Chapter 22

The Revelation of the Spirit

And my speech and my preaching were not with persuasive words of human wisdom, but in demonstration of the Spirit and of power, that your faith should not be in the wisdom of men but in the power of God. However, we speak wisdom among those who are mature, yet not the wisdom of this age, nor of the rulers of this age, who are coming to nothing. But we speak the wisdom of God in a mystery, the hidden wisdom which God ordained before the ages for our glory, which none of the rulers of this age knew. . . . But God has revealed them to us through His Spirit. For the Spirit searches all things, yes, the deep things of God. Now we have received, not the spirit of the world, but the Spirit who is from God, that we might know the things that have been freely given to us by God. These things we also speak, not in words which man's wisdom teaches but which the Holy Spirit teaches, comparing spiritual things with spiritual. But the natural man does not receive the things of the Spirit of God, for they are foolishness to him; nor can he know them, because they are spiritually discerned. But he who is spiritual judges all things, yet he himself is rightly judged by no one.

1 Corinthians 2:4–8, 10, 12–15

In this passage Paul contrasts the spirit of the world and the Spirit of God. The point at which the contrast particularly is seen is in the wisdom or knowledge of the truth. It was in seeking knowledge that man fell. It was in the pride of knowledge that heathenism had its origin: "Professing to be wise, they became fools" (Romans 1:22). It was in wisdom, philosophy, and the search after truth that the Greeks sought glory. It was in the knowledge of God's will: "having the form of knowledge and truth in the law" (Romans 2:20) that the Jew made his boast. And yet when Christ, the wisdom of God, appeared on earth, both Jew and Greek rejected Him. Man's wisdom, whether or not in possession of a revelation, is utterly insufficient for comprehending God or His wisdom. Just as his heart is alienated from God so that he does not love His will or do it, so his mind is darkened so that he cannot know Him aright. Even when in Christ the light of God's divine love shone upon men, they knew it not and saw no beauty in it.

In the epistle to the Romans, Paul dealt with man's trust in his own righteousness and its insufficiency. To the Corinthians, especially in the first three chapters, he exposes the insufficiency of man's wisdom. Not merely when it was a question of discovering God's truth and will, as with the Greeks, but even where God had revealed it, as with the Jews, man was incapable of seeing it without divine illumination—the light of the Holy Spirit. The rulers of this world, Jew and Gentile, crucified the Lord of glory because they didn't have the wisdom of God. In writing to believers at Corinth, and warning them against the wisdom of the world, Paul is not dealing with any heresy, Jewish or heathen. He is speaking to believers who had fully accepted his gospel of a crucified Christ, but who were in danger, in preaching or hearing the truth, of dealing with it in the power of human wisdom. He reminds them that the truth of God, as a hidden spiritual mystery, can be comprehended only by a spiritual revelation. The rejection of Christ by the Jews was proof of the utter incapacity of human wisdom to grasp a divine revelation without the spiritual, internal illumination of the Holy Spirit.

The Jews prided themselves on their attachment to God's Word, their study of it, their conformity to it in life and conduct. The issue proved that, without their being conscious of it, they utterly misunderstood it and rejected the very Messiah for whom they thought they were waiting. Divine revelation, as Paul expounds it in this chapter, means three things: (1) God must make known in His Word what He thinks and does. (2) Every preacher who is to communicate the message must not only be in possession of the truth but continually be taught by the Spirit how to speak it. (3) Every hearer needs the inward illumination: It is only as he is a spiritual man, with his life under the rule of the Spirit, that his mind can take in spiritual truth. As we have the mind and the disposition of Christ, we can discern the truth as it is in Christ Jesus.

This teaching is what the church in our day, and each believer in particular, needs. With the Reformation, the insufficiency of man's righteousness and of his power to fulfill God's law obtained universal recognition in the Reformed churches and, in theory at least, is everywhere accepted among evangelical Christians. The insufficiency of man's wisdom has by no means obtained as clear a recognition. While the need of the Holy Spirit's teaching is in general willingly admitted, we find that neither in the teaching of the church nor in the lives of believers does this blessed truth have practical and all-embracing supremacy—without which the wisdom and spirit of this world will continue to assert its power.

The proof of what we have said will be found in what Paul says of his own preaching: "And my speech and my preaching were not with persuasive words of human wisdom, but in demonstration of the Spirit and of power" (1 Corinthians 2:4). He is not writing, as to the Galatians, of two gospels, but of two ways of preaching the one gospel of Christ's cross. He says that to preach it in persuasive words of man's wisdom produces a faith that will bear the mark of its origin—a faith in the wisdom of man. As long as it is nourished by men and means, it may stand and flourish. But it cannot stand alone or in the day of trial. A man may with such preaching become a believer, but he will be a weak believer. The faith, on the other hand, received as a result of preaching in the Spirit and power, stands in the power of God. The believer is led by the preaching, by the Holy Spirit himself, beyond man, into direct contact with the living God; his faith stands in the power of God. As long as the great majority of our church members, even though there is an abundance of the means of grace, are in a weak and sickly state, with little of the faith that stands in the power of God, we must suspect that it is because too much of our preaching is more in the wisdom of man than in the demonstration of the power of the Spirit. If a change is to take effect both in the spirit in which our preachers and teachers speak and our congregations listen and receive, it must begin in the personal life of the individual believer.

We must learn to question our own wisdom: "Trust in the Lord with all your heart, and lean not on your own understanding" (Proverbs 3:5–6). Paul says to believers: "If anyone among you seems to be wise in this age, let him become a fool that he may become wise" (1 Corinthians 3:18). When Scripture tells us that they that are Christ's have crucified the flesh, this includes the understanding of the flesh, the fleshly mind of which Scripture speaks. Just as in the crucifixion of self I give up my own goodness, my own strength, my own will to death because there is no good in it, and look to Christ by the power of His life to give me the goodness and the strength and the will that is pleasing to God, so it must be also with my own wisdom. Man's mind is one of his noblest and most godlike faculties. But sin rules over it and in it. A man may be truly converted and yet not know to what extent he is trying to grasp and keep the truth of God with his natural mind. The reason that there is so much Bible reading and teaching that has no power to elevate and sanctify the life is simply this: It is not truth that has been revealed and received through the Holy Spirit.

This also goes for truth that has once been taught us by the Holy Spirit, but which, having been lodged in the understanding, is now held simply by the memory. Manna speedily loses its heavenliness when stored up on earth. Truth received from heaven loses its divine freshness unless the anointing with fresh oil is there every day. The believer needs, day by day, hour by hour, to know that there is nothing in which the power of the flesh can assert itself more insidiously than in the activity of the mind or reason in its dealing with the divine Word. This will cause one to realize that he must continually seek, in Paul's language, "to become a fool." Each time he deals with God's Word or thinks of God's truth, He needs in faith and teachableness to wait for the interpretation of the Spirit. He needs to ask for the "circumcised ear"—from which the fleshly power of understanding has been removed. To such this word will be fulfilled: "I thank You, Father, Lord of heaven and earth, that You have hidden these things from the wise and prudent and have revealed them to babes" (Matthew 11:25).

The question for all pastors and teachers, professors and theologians, students and readers of the Bible, is a serious one. Do you know that there must be perfect correspondence between the objective spiritual contents of the revelation and the subjective spiritual apprehension of it on our part? Between our apprehension of it and our communication of it—both in the power of the Holy Spirit? And then between our communication of it and the reception of it by those who hear us? Our halls of theological study, seminaries, and Bible training institutes need a banner over them with the words of Paul: "God has revealed it unto us by His Holy Spirit." Pastors must influence and train their people to see that it is not the amount or the clarity or the interesting aspect of Bible knowledge received that will determine the blessing and the power, but the measure of dependence upon the Holy Spirit that accompanies it. God will honor those who honor Him. Nowhere will this word be found more true than here. The crucifixion of self and its wisdom, the coming in weakness and holy fear, as Paul did, will be met with the demonstration of the Spirit and of power.

It is not enough that the light of Christ shines on you in the Word; the light of the Spirit must shine *in* you. Each time you come in contact with the Word through study, preaching, or reading Christian literature, there ought to be an act of self-denial, a choice to deny your own wisdom, yielding yourself in faith to the divine Teacher. Affirm that He dwells within you. Rejoice in renewing your surrender to Him. Reject the spirit of the world with its wisdom and self-confidence; come in poverty of spirit to be led by the Spirit of God. "Do not be conformed to this world, but be transformed by the renewing of your mind, that you may prove what is that good and acceptable and perfect will of God" (Romans 12:2). It is a transformed, renewed life that wants only to know God's perfect will that will be taught by the Spirit. Cease from your own wisdom; wait for the wisdom of the Spirit, which God has promised. You will increasingly be able to testify of the things that have not entered into the hearts of men to conceive, because God has revealed them to you by His Spirit.

O God, I praise you for the wondrous revelation of yourself in Christ crucified, the wisdom of God and the power of God. And that while man's wisdom leaves him helpless in the presence of the power of sin and death, Christ crucified proves that He is the wisdom of God by the mighty redemption He works. I thank you that what He worked and bestowed as our Savior is revealed to us by the divine light of your own Holy Spirit.

We ask that you teach your church that wherever Christ

as the power of God is not manifested, it is because He is so little known as the wisdom of God. Teach your church to lead each child of God to the personal teaching and revelation of Christ within.

Show us, O God, that the greatest hindrance is our own wisdom, our imagining that we can understand the Word and truth of God on our own. Teach us to become fools that we may be wise. Make our life a continual act of faith that the Holy Spirit will do His work of teaching, guiding, and leading into all truth. Father, you gave Him that He might reveal Jesus within us; we wait for this. Amen.

Summary

1. "God has chosen the foolish things of the world to put to shame the wise" (1 Corinthians 1:27). (Compare 1:19–21; 3:19–20.) Was it only at Corinth that believers needed this teaching? Or is there not in every man a wisdom that is not of God, and a readiness to think that he can understand the Word without direct contact with the living God? This wisdom seeks to master even the most spiritual truth, to form a clear concept or image of it, and boasts in that instead of the revelation of the Spirit.

2. Jesus had the spirit of wisdom. How did it manifest itself? In His waiting to hear what the Father spoke. Perfect teachableness was the mark of the Son on earth. This is the mark of the Spirit in us. As the Spirit finds our life in obedience to Him, He teaches us through what He works in us.

3. It is inconceivable, until God reveals it to us, how a Christian can deceive himself with the semblance of wis-

dom in lofty thoughts and affecting sentiments while the *power* of God is lacking. The *wisdom* of man stands in contrast to the power of God. The only true sign of divine wisdom is its power. The kingdom of God is not mere words and thoughts and knowledge, but power. May God open our eyes to see how much of our Christianity consists in impressive words, thoughts, and feelings, but not in the power of God.

4. Note that the spirit of the world and the wisdom of the world are one. The extent to which many Christians yield themselves to the influence of the literature of the age without fear or caution, is one of the great reasons why the Holy Spirit cannot guide them or reveal Christ in them.

Chapter 23

Are You
Spiritual or Carnal?

*And I, brethren, could not speak to you as to spiritual
people but as to carnal, as to babes in Christ. I fed you
with milk and not with solid food; for until now you were
not able to receive it, and even now you are still not able;
for you are still carnal. For where there are envy, strife,
and divisions among you, are you not carnal
and behaving like mere men?*

1 Corinthians 3:1–3

If we live in the Spirit, let us also walk in the Spirit.

Galatians 5:25

In the previous chapter the apostle contrasts the believer as
the spiritual man with the unregenerate as the natural (or
psychical) man; the man of the Spirit with the man of the
soul (1 Corinthians 2:14–15). Here he supplements that
teaching. He tells the Corinthians that though they have the
Spirit, he cannot call them spiritual; that title belongs to

those who have not only received the Spirit but have yielded themselves to Him to rule their life. Those who have not done this, in whom the power of the flesh is still more manifest than the Spirit, cannot be called spiritual, but carnal. There are three states in which a man may be found. The unregenerate is still the natural man, not having the Spirit of God. The regenerate, who is still a babe in Christ—either recently converted or not progressing—is the carnal man, giving way to the power of the flesh. The believer in whom the Spirit has obtained full supremacy is the spiritual man. The whole passage contains rich instruction with regard to the life of the Spirit within us.

The young Christian is still carnal. Regeneration is a birth: the center and root of the personality, the spirit, has been renewed and taken possession of by the Spirit of God. But time is needed for its power from that center to extend throughout the whole being. The kingdom of God is like a seed; the life in Christ is a growth; and it would be against the laws of nature and grace alike if we expected from the babe in Christ the strength that can be found only in grown men, or the rich experience of the fathers. Even where there is great singleness of heart and faith in the young convert with true love and devotion to the Savior, time is needed for a deeper knowledge of self and sin, for a spiritual insight into what God's will and grace are. With the young believer it is not unnatural that the emotions are deeply stirred and that the mind delights in the contemplation of divine truth. With growth in grace, the will becomes the more important thing; waiting for the Spirit's power in the life and character means more than the delight in those thoughts and images of life that the mind alone can offer. We need not wonder if the babe in Christ is still carnal.

Many Christians remain carnal. God has not only called us to grow, but has provided all the conditions and powers needful for growth. And yet it is sadly true that there are many Christians who, like the Corinthians, remain babes in Christ when they ought to be going on to perfection, attaining unto full-grown men. In some cases the blame is almost more with the church and its teaching than with individuals. When the preaching makes salvation seem to consist only in pardon and peace and the hope of heaven, or when, if a holy life is preached, the truth of Christ our sanctification, our sufficiency for holiness, and the Holy Spirit's indwelling are not taught clearly and in the power of the Spirit, growth can hardly be expected. Ignorance, and human and defective views of the gospel as the power of God unto a present salvation in sanctification are the cause of the error.

In other cases, the root of the error is to be found in the unwillingness of the Christian to deny self and crucify the flesh. The call of Jesus to every disciple is to deny himself and take up his cross and follow Him. The Spirit is given only to the obedient. He can do His work only in those who are absolutely willing to submit self to death. The sins that proved the Corinthians were carnal were jealousy and strife. When Christians are not willing to give up the sin of selfishness and willfulness; when—whether in family relationships or in the wider circle of the church and public life—they want to retain the freedom of giving in to or excusing evil feelings, of pronouncing their own judgments, and speaking words that are not in perfect love, they remain carnal. With all their knowledge, their practice of the Christian disciplines, and their work for God's kingdom, they can still be carnal and not spiritual. They grieve the Holy Spirit of God; they do not have the testimony that they are pleasing to God.

The carnal Christian cannot appropriate spiritual truth. Paul writes to these Corinthians: "I fed you with milk and not with solid food; for until now you were not able to receive it, and even now you are still not able." The Corinthians prided themselves on their wisdom; Paul thanked God that they were "enriched in all knowledge." There was nothing in His teaching that they would not have been able to comprehend with their natural understanding. But spiritual entrance into the truth in power—so as to possess it and be possessed by it, so as to have not only the thoughts but the truth the words speak—this only the Holy Spirit can give. He gives it only to the spiritually minded. The teaching and leading of the Spirit is given to the obedient and is preceded by the leading of the Spirit in putting to death the deeds of the body (see Romans 8:13–14). Spiritual knowledge is not deep thought but living contact, entering into and being united to the truth as it is in Jesus, a spiritual reality, a substantive existence. Into a spiritual mind the Spirit works spiritual truth. It is not the power of intellect, or even the earnest desire to know the truth that equips a man for the Spirit's teaching. It is a life yielded to Him—in dependence and full obedience—to be made spiritual that receives the spiritual wisdom and understanding. In the mind (the will) these two elements—the moral and the cognitive—are united; only as the former has precedence and influence can the latter apprehend what God has spoken.

It is easy to understand how a carnal life with its walk, and a worldly mind with its knowledge, act and react on each other. As long as we are yielding to the flesh, we are incapable of receiving spiritual insight into truth. We may "understand all mysteries and all knowledge," but without love—the love that the Spirit works in the inner life—it is only a knowledge that puffs up; it profits nothing. The carnal life makes the knowledge carnal. And this knowledge, again, being thus held in the fleshly mind, strengthens the religion of the flesh, self-trust and self-effort; the truth so received has no power to renew and make free. No wonder there is so much Bible teaching and Bible knowledge with so little resultant holiness in lives. I pray that His Word might speak to His church: "Where there is among you envy and strife, are you not carnal?" Unless we are living spiritual lives—full of humility, love, and self-sacrifice— spiritual truth, the truth of God, cannot enter or benefit us.

Every Christian is called of God to be spiritual. Paul reproves these Corinthians, who were only recently brought out of heathenism, that they are not yet spiritual. The object of redemption in Christ is the removal of every hindrance so that the Spirit of God might be able to make one's heart and life a worthy home for God who is Spirit. That redemption was not a failure; the Holy Spirit came down to inaugurate a new, yet unknown, dispensation of His indwelling life and power. The promise and love of the Father, the power and the glory of the Son, the presence of the Spirit on earth—are promises and guarantees that it is possible. As surely as the natural man can become a regenerate man, so can a regenerate man who is still carnal become spiritual.

Why is it then not always so? This question brings us to the unfathomable mystery of the choice that God has given us to accept or refuse His offer; to be faithful or not to the grace He has given. We have already spoken of that failure on the part of the church in its defective teaching of the indwelling and the sanctifying power of the Holy Spirit in the believer, and on the part of believers in their unwillingness to forsake all and allow the Holy Spirit to take full possession of them. Let us look again at what Scripture teaches as to how to become spiritual.

It is the Holy Spirit who makes the spiritual man, but only where the individual is yielded to Him. To have our whole being pervaded, influenced, sanctified by the Holy Spirit, we must first have our spirit, soul—will, feelings, mind—and body under His control, moved and guided by Him. This makes and seals the spiritual man.

The first step on the way to true spirituality is faith. We must seek the living, all-consuming conviction that the Holy Spirit is in us; that He is the power of God dwelling and working within us, that He is the representative of Jesus, making Him present within us as our Redeemer King, mighty to save. In the union of a holy fear and reverence before the tremendous glory of this truth of an indwelling God, with the childlike joy and trust of knowing Him as the Paraclete, the bringer of the divine and irrevocable presence of Christ, this thought must become the inspiration of our life: The Holy Spirit has made His home within us; in our spirit is His hidden, blessed dwelling place.

As we are filled with faith in what He is and will do, we will seek to know the hindrance if it is not accomplished.

But we find that there is an opposing power: our own flesh. From Scripture we learn how the flesh offends in two ways: unrighteousness and self-righteousness. Both must be confessed and surrendered to Him whom the Spirit would reveal and enthrone as Lord and Savior. All that is carnal and sinful, every work of the flesh, must be given up and cast out—all self-effort and striving. The soul, with all its powers, must be brought into subjection to Jesus Christ. In deep and daily dependence upon God, we must accept, wait for, and follow the Holy Spirit.

Walking in faith and obedience, we may count on the Holy Spirit to do a divine and blessed work within us. By faith we live in the Spirit, we walk in the Spirit, yielding ourselves to His mighty working in us to will and to do all that is pleasing in God's sight.

Gracious God, we humbly pray that you will teach us all to benefit from the deep lessons of this portion of your blessed Word.

Fill us with a holy fear and reverence, lest with all our knowledge of the truth of Christ and the Spirit we should be carnal in disposition and conduct, not walking in the love and purity of your Holy Spirit. May we understand that knowledge puffs up, unless it is under the rule of the love that builds up.

May we hear your call to be spiritual, by your Holy Spirit to manifest the fruits of the Spirit and be conformed to the likeness of Christ Jesus.

Strengthen our faith! Fill us with confidence that the Holy Spirit will do His work to make us spiritual. We yield ourselves to our Lord to rule in us, to reveal himself by His Spirit.

We bow before you in childlike faith that your Spirit will dwell in us every moment. May our souls increasingly be filled with awe at His presence. According to the riches of your glory, grant that we might be strengthened by Him in the inner man. Only then will we be truly spiritual. Amen.

Summary

1. All believers must rise from the carnal stage to the spiritual stage of the Christian life, where the Spirit of Pentecost has reign and rule.

2. To understand the word *carnal* and the life Paul condemns so strongly here, compare Romans 7:14, "I am carnal, sold under sin," and the description of the hopeless and undelivered state of which that word is the secret. To understand the word *spiritual,* compare Romans 8:6, "to be spiritually minded is life and peace," with the description of the life of the Spirit in the context (vv. 2–16). Compare also Galatians 5:15–16, 22, 25–26, and 6:1, to see that being *carnal* is lacking in love, while being *spiritual* exhibits the meekness and love that keeps the new commandment.

3. When a man is regenerated, the new life within is only a seed, in the midst of a body of sin and flesh, with its carnal wisdom and will. In that seed there is Christ and His Spirit as the power of God in us; but because a seed is a frail thing, it may be overlooked or distrusted. Faith knows the mighty power that there is in that seed to overcome the world and bring the whole being and life into subjection. So the Spirit rules and conquers and enables the man to put to death the deeds of the flesh and become spiritual.

4. The fact that true spiritual insight into God's Word depends upon a spiritual life is one of supreme importance for pastors and teachers of the Word. Let us pray for the leaders of the church that they may be spiritual. It is not the soundness of the teaching itself or the earnestness of the teacher, but the power of the Spirit that makes one's thoughts and words spiritual.

Chapter 24

The Temple
of the Holy Spirit

*Do you not know that you are the temple of God and that
the Spirit of God dwells in you?*

1 Corinthians 3:16

Scripture invites us to study the analogy of the temple and the Holy Spirit's indwelling. The temple was constructed according to a pattern that Moses saw on the Mount, a shadow cast by the eternal spiritual realities it symbolized. One of these realities is man's threefold nature. Because man was created in the image of God, the temple is not only an example of the mystery of man's approach into the presence of God, but equally of God's way of entering into man, to take up residence with him.

We are familiar with the division of the temple into three parts. There was the exterior, seen by all men, with the outer court into which every Israelite could enter and where all the external services were performed. There was the holy place, into which only the priests could enter, to present to God the blood or the incense, the bread or the oil, that they had brought from outside. Although near, they were still not within the veil; into the immediate presence of God. God dwelled in the holiest of all, in a light inaccessible, where none might venture. The momentary entering of the high priest once a year was only to make them conscious of the truth that there was no place for man there until the veil was rent in two.

Man is God's temple. In him there are three parts. The body represents the outer court, the external, visible life, where the conduct is regulated by God's law and where all service consists in looking at how things are around us and for bringing us close to God. The soul represents the inner life, the power of the mind and feeling and will. In the regenerate man this is the holy place, where thoughts and affections and desires move to and fro as the priests of the sanctuary, rendering God their service in the full light of consciousness. Then there is, within the veil, hidden from all human sight and light, the hidden innermost sanctuary, the secret place of the Most High, where God dwells and where man may not enter, until the veil is rent. Man has not only body and soul but also spirit. Deeper than the soul with its consciousness, there is the spirit-nature linking man with God. So great is sin's power that in some this part dies: They are sensual, not having the Spirit. In others, it is nothing more than a dormant place, a void waiting for the quickening of the Holy Spirit. In the believer, it is the inner chamber of the heart, of which the Spirit has taken possession, and out of which He waits to do His glorious work, making soul and body holy unto the Lord.

However, unless this indwelling is recognized, yielded

to, and humbly maintained in adoration and love, it will bring comparatively little blessing. Acknowledging the indwelling presence of the Holy Spirit will enable us to regard the whole temple, even to the outmost court, as sacred to His service, and to yield every facet of our nature to His leading and will. The most sacred part of the temple—for which all the rest existed and depended—was the Holy of Holies. Even though the priests might never enter and see the glory that dwelt there, their conduct was regulated and their faith motivated by the thought of the unseen presence it contained. It was this fact that gave the sprinkling of the blood and the burning of the incense value. And it was this fact that made it a privilege to draw nigh and that gave them confidence to go out and to bless the people. It was the Holy of Holies that made the place where they served a holy place. Their whole life was controlled and inspired by faith in the unseen indwelling glory within the veil.

And so it is with the believer. Until he learns by faith to bow in holy fear at the wondrous mystery that he is God's temple because God's Spirit dwells in him, he will never accept his high vocation with the joyful confidence it deserves. As long as he looks only at the holy place as far as man can see on his own, he will search in vain for the Holy Spirit. Each must learn to know the secret place of the most high within.

How is this faith in the hidden indwelling to become ours? Taking a stand upon God's Word and accepting and appropriating its teaching. We must believe that God means what He says. We are His temple—a type of the temple God commanded to be built. He wants us to see in it what God intended for us. The Holy of Holies was the central point, the essential portion of the temple. It was dark, secret, hidden, until the time of its unveiling. It demanded and received the faith of the priest and the people. The holiest of all within me is unseen and hidden, too, at first—something for faith alone to pursue and know. The Father and the Son even now make their home within me. I will meditate and be still until something of the overwhelming glory of this truth dawns upon me and faith begins to realize that I am His temple, and in the secret place He sits upon His throne. As I yield myself in meditation and worship day by day, surrendering and opening my whole being to Him, He will in His divine, loving, living power shine into my consciousness the light of His presence.

Amid the terrible experience of failure and sin new hope will break through. Though I may have earnestly sought to do so, I could not keep the holy place for God, because He keeps it himself. If I give Him the glory due His name, He will send forth His light and His truth through my whole being, revealing His power to sanctify and to bless. Through the soul, coming ever more securely under His rule, His power will work, even in the passions and appetites within, with every thought made subject to the Holy Spirit.

If you have put away sin and asked the Spirit to dwell in you, believe that He does and that you are the temple of the living God! You have been sealed with the Holy Spirit; He is the assurance of your Father's love.

Remember that the veil was but for a time. When the preparation was complete, the veil of the flesh was rent. Just as Christ's death rent the veil of the temple, so the veil is rent in you to allow the entrance of the most Holy Spirit into your being. The hidden glory of the secret place will pour into your conscious life: the service of the holy place will be in the power of the eternal Spirit.

Most Holy God, in adoring wonder I bow before you in the presence of this wondrous mystery of grace: My spirit, soul, and body are your temple.

In deep silence and worship I accept the blessed revelation that in me, too, there is a holiest of all and that there your hidden glory has its home.

Forgive me that I have known so little of it. But now I accept the blessed truth: God the Spirit, the Holy Spirit, who is God himself, dwells in me.

Father, reveal what it means, lest I sin against you by speaking of it and not living it. I yield my whole being to you. I trust in you and your power to have your way within me.

I believe in you for the full pouring forth of the living waters. You, holy Teacher, mighty Sanctifier, are within me. On you I wait all the day. I belong to you. Take entire possession of me for the sake of the Father and the Son. Amen.

Summary

1. The *spirit* here (John 4:24) denotes that deepest element of the human soul by which it can hold communion with God. It is the seat of self-control, the sanctuary wherein true worship is celebrated (Romans 1:9).
2. Note how Paul, in appealing to the Corinthians to rise out of their deep carnal state, more than once pleads with them on the ground of their being temples of the Holy Spirit. In our day, many think the indwelling of the

Holy Spirit ought to be preached only to more mature Christians. Let us learn here that every believer has the Holy Spirit, that he ought to know it, and that knowing it is the most effective tool for rising up out of a carnal life and coming into the fullness of the Spirit. Let us work to bring every believer to an awareness of this, his heavenly birthright.

3. It is the body that is the temple of the Holy Spirit (1 Corinthians 6:19). If our spirit is filled with the Spirit of God, it will manifest itself in the body, too. "If by the Spirit you put to death the deeds of the body, you will live" (Romans 8:13). Let us believe that the divine Spirit is particularly given to pervade, to purify, and to strengthen our bodies for His service. It is His indwelling in the body that makes it a living seed that shares in the resurrection life.

4. Do you know it by faith? Are you pressing on to know it in full experience so that your deepest consciousness will spontaneously say, *Yes, I am a temple of God; the Spirit of God dwells in me. Glory be to His name!*

Chapter 25

The Ministry
of the Spirit

*Not that we are sufficient of ourselves to think of anything
as being from ourselves, but our sufficiency is from God,
who also made us sufficient as ministers of the new
covenant, not of the letter but of the Spirit; for the letter
kills, but the Spirit gives life. But if the ministry of
death . . . was glorious . . . how will the ministry
of the Spirit not be more glorious?*

2 Corinthians 3:5–8

In none of his epistles does Paul expound his concept of
the Christian ministry so clearly and fully as in the second
epistle to the Corinthians. The need of vindicating his apos-
tleship against detractors, the consciousness of divine
power and glory working in him in the midst of weakness,
the intense longing of his loving heart to communicate
what he had to impart, stirs his soul to its very depths, and
he lays open to us the inmost secrets of the life that makes
one a true minister of Christ and His Spirit. In our text, we

have the central thought: Paul finds his sufficiency of strength, the inspiration and rule of all his conduct, in the fact that he has been made a minister of the Spirit. If we take the various passages in which mention is made of the Holy Spirit in the first half of the epistle (through to 6:10), we shall see what, in his view, is the place and work of the Holy Spirit in the ministry and what is the character of a ministry under His leading and in His power.

In this epistle, Paul speaks with authority. He begins by placing himself on a level with his readers. In his first mention of the Spirit, he tells them that the Spirit who is in him is none other than the One who is in them. "Now He who establishes us with you in Christ and has anointed us is God, who also has sealed us and given us the Spirit in our hearts as a guarantee" (1:21–22). The anointing of the believer with the Spirit, bringing him into fellowship with Christ and revealing what He is to us; the sealing, setting him apart as God's own and giving him assurance of it; the earnest of the Spirit, securing at once the foretaste and the equipping for the heavenly inheritance in glory: of all this they are partakers together. In spite of whatever there was among the Corinthians that was wrong or unholy, Paul speaks to them, thinks of them, and loves them as one in Christ. This deep sense of unity fills his soul, comes out throughout the epistle, and is the secret of his influence. See 1:6, 10; 2:3: "I wrote this very thing to you . . . having confidence in you all that my joy is the joy of you all"; 4:5: "ourselves your bondservants"; 4:10–12: "carrying about in the body the dying of the Lord Jesus . . . that the life of Jesus also may be manifested in our mortal flesh"; 4:15: "all things are for your sakes"; 6:11, 7:3: "our heart is wide open ... to die together and to live together." If the unity of the Spirit, the consciousness of being members one of another, is necessary in all believers, how much more should it be the mark of those who are leaders? The power of the ministry to the saints depends upon the unity of the Spirit, the full recognition of believers as partakers of the anointing. But to this end the minister must himself live as an anointed and sealed one, showing that he has the earnest of the Spirit in his heart.

The second passage is 2 Corinthians 3:3: "You are an epistle of Christ, ministered by us, written not with ink but by the Spirit of the living God, not on tablets of stone but on tablets of flesh, that is, of the heart." As distinct an act of God as was the writing of the law on the tables of stone, so is the writing of the law of the Spirit in the new covenant, and of the name of Christ on the heart. It is a divine work, in which, as truly as God wrote of old, the Holy Spirit uses the tongue of His minister as His pen. It is this truth that needs to be restored in the ministry, not only that the Holy Spirit is needed, but that He waits to do the work, and will do it, when the right relationship to Him is maintained. Paul's own experience at Corinth (Acts 18:5–11; 1 Corinthians 2:3) teaches us what conscious weakness, what fear, what sense of absolute helplessness is needed if the power of God is to rest upon us. The whole epistle confirms this: It was as a man under sentence of death, bearing about the dying of the Lord Jesus that the power of Christ worked in him. The Spirit of God stands in contrast to the flesh, the world, the self, with its life and strength; it is as these are broken down and the flesh has nothing to glory in that the Spirit will work.

Then come the words of our text (3:6–7), to teach us what the special characteristic is of this new covenant ministry of the Spirit: It "gives life." The antithesis, "the letter kills," applies not only to the law of the Old Testament, but, according to the teaching of Scripture, to all knowledge that is not in the quickening power of the Spirit. We cannot insist upon it too earnestly that, even as the law, though we know it was "spiritual," so the gospel, too, has its letter. The gospel may be preached most clearly and faithfully; it may exert a strong moral influence; and yet the faith that comes of it may stand in the wisdom of men and not in the power of God. If there is one thing the church needs to cry for on behalf of its ministers and students, it is that the ministry of the Spirit may be restored in its full power. Pray that God may teach them what it is to personally live in the sealing, the anointing, the assurance of the indwelling Spirit; what it is to know that the letter kills but the Spirit gives life; and to know, above all, that the personal life is under the ministry of the Spirit so that He can freely work.

Paul now proceeds to contrast the two dispensations and the different characters of those who live in them. He points out how, as long as the mind is blinded, there is a veil on the heart that can only be taken away as we turn to the Lord. And then he adds (3:17–18): "Now the Lord is the Spirit; and where the Spirit of the Lord is, there is liberty. But we all, with unveiled face, beholding as in a mirror the glory of the Lord, are being transformed into the same image from glory to glory, just as by the Spirit of the Lord." It was when our Lord Jesus was exalted into the life of the Spirit that He sent His Holy Spirit to His people. The disciples knew Jesus in the flesh, without knowing Him as the

Spirit of the Lord. Paul speaks of this, too, with regard to his knowing Christ in the flesh for a season (2 Corinthians 5:16). There may be a lot of earnest preaching of the Lord Jesus as the crucified one, without preaching Him as the Spirit of the Lord. It is only as the latter truth is apprehended and experienced that the double blessing of which Paul speaks will come: "Where the Spirit of the Lord is, there is liberty." Believers will be led into the glorious liberty of the children of God (Romans 8:2; Galatians 5:1, 18). Then will He do the work for which He was sent—to reveal the glory of the Lord in us; and as we behold it, we shall be changed from glory to glory. Of the time before Pentecost it was written that the Spirit was not yet because Jesus was not yet glorified. But when He had been received up into glory, the Spirit came forth into our hearts, that we with unveiled face, beholding the glory of the Lord, might be changed into His likeness. What a calling! the ministry of the Spirit! to hold up the glory of the Lord to His redeemed, and to be used by His Spirit in working their transformation into His likeness, from glory to glory. Where there is clear knowledge of Christ as Lord and the Spirit of Christ as changing believers into His likeness, ministry among believers will be in life and power—a ministry of the Spirit.

The power of the ministry on the divine side is the Spirit, and on the human side, faith. The next mention of the Spirit is in 4:13: Having "the same spirit of faith." After having, in chapter 3, set forth the glory of the ministry of the Spirit, and in chapter 4:1–6, the glory of the gospel preached, he turns to the vessels in which this treasure is. He has to vindicate his apparent weakness. But he does far more. Instead of apologizing for it, he expounds its divine meaning and glory. He proves how this situation constituted his power, because in his weakness divine power could work. It has been so ordained "that the excellence of the power may be of God and not of us" (v. 7). So his perfect fellowship with Jesus was maintained as he carried "about in the body the dying of the Lord Jesus, that the life of Jesus also may be manifested in our body" (v. 10). So there was even in his sufferings something of the vicarious element that marked his Lord's: "So then death is working in us, but life in you" (v. 12). And then he adds, as the expression of the animating power that sustained him through all endurance and labor: "And since we have the same spirit of faith," of which we read in the Scripture, "according to what is written, 'I believed, and therefore I spoke'; we also believe and therefore speak, knowing that He who raised up the Lord Jesus will also raise us up with Jesus, and will present us with you" (vv. 13–14).

Faith is the evidence of things not seen. It sees the invisible and lives in it. Beginning with trust in Jesus, "Though now you do not see Him, yet believing, you rejoice with joy inexpressible and full of glory" (1 Peter 1:8), it goes on through the whole of the Christian life. Whatever is of the Spirit is by faith. The great work of God, in opening the heart of His child to receive more of the Spirit, is to school his faith into more perfect freedom from all that is seen, and the more complete rest in God, even to the assurance that God dwells and works mightily in his weakness. For this reason trials and sufferings are sent. Paul uses very remarkable language in regard to his sufferings in 2 Corinthians 1:9: "We had the sentence of death in ourselves, that we should not trust in ourselves but in God who raises the dead." Even Paul was in danger of trusting in himself. Nothing is more natural; all life is confident of self, and nature is consistent with itself until it dies. For the mighty work he had to do, he needed a trust in no one less than the living God, who raises the dead. To this God led him by giving him, in the affliction that came upon him in Asia, the sentence of death in himself. The trial of his faith was its strength. In our context he returns to this thought: The fellowship of the dying of Jesus is to him the means and the assurance of the experience of the power of Christ's life. In the spirit of this faith he speaks: "who delivered us from so great a death, and does deliver us; in whom we trust that He will still deliver us" (1:10).

It was not until Jesus had died that the Spirit of life could break forth from Him. The life of Jesus was born out of the grave: It is a life out of death. It is as we daily die, and carry with us the dying of Jesus; as flesh and self are mortified; as we have in ourselves God's sentence of death on all that is of self and flesh—that the life and the Spirit of Jesus will be manifest in us. And this is the Spirit of faith, that in the midst of weakness and apparent death, it depends on God who raises the dead. This is the ministry of the Spirit—when faith glories in infirmities—that the power of Christ may rest upon it. As our faith does not stagger at the earthly weakness of the vessel, as it consents to the fact that the excellency of the power shall not be of ourselves but of God, then the Spirit will work in the power of the living God.

We find the same thought in the two remaining passages. In 5:5, he speaks again of "the Spirit as a guarantee" in connection with our groaning and being burdened. And then in 6:6–10, the Spirit is introduced in the midst of the mention of his distresses and labors as the mark of his ministry: "In all things we commend ourselves as ministers of God: in much patience, in tribulations ... *by the Holy Spirit* ... as dying, and behold we live; as chastened and yet not killed; as sorrowful, yet always rejoicing; as poor, yet making many rich." The power of Christ in the Holy Spirit was to Paul such a living reality that the weakness of the flesh only led him to more fully rejoice and trust in it. The Holy Spirit's dwelling and working in him was the secret spring and the divine power of his ministry.

We may well ask, "Does the Holy Spirit take the place in our ministry that He did in Paul's?" There is not a minister or member of the church who does not have a vital interest in the answer. The question is not whether we submit to the doctrine of the absolute need of the Holy Spirit's working, but whether we give to securing His presence a commensurate proportion of our time, our thoughts, and our faith. Does the Holy Spirit have the place in the church that the Lord Jesus desires Him to have? When our hearts are opened to the glorious truth that He is the power of God, that in Him Christ works through us, and that He is the presence of the glorified Lord, we will agree that the need of the church is to wait at the foot of the throne for the clothing with power from on high. The Spirit of Christ, in the power of His life and death, is the spirit of the ministry. As the church grasps this, it will be what the Head of the church meant it to be: the ministry of the Spirit.

Blessed Father, we thank you for the institution of the ministry of the Word as the great means through which our exalted Lord does His saving work by the Holy Spirit. We thank you that it is a ministry of the Spirit and for all the blessing you have wrought through it in the world. Our prayer is that you would increasingly make it throughout your church what you would have it to be—a ministry of the Spirit and of power.

Help us to know how much we still fall short of your purposes. Reveal to us how much we trust in our flesh, our own zeal and strength, the wisdom of this world. Teach us all the secret of giving place to the Spirit of Christ that He may use us as fit vessels to teach others. Amen.

Summary

1. Christ needed to be made perfect through suffering. It was through suffering He entered the glory out of which the Spirit was sent. He was crucified in weakness, yet He lives through the power of God. Paul could not exercise his ministry of the Spirit in power without the continual experience of the same weakness. So death works in us, but life in you. We are also weak in Him, but will live with Him through the gift of God toward you. With martyrs and missionaries, persecution and tribulation have been the fellowship of Christ's suffering and weakness, His power and Spirit. We may invite neither persecution nor suffering, but we may enter into the needs and the sorrows of those suffering around us.

2. The standard of the ministry and that of the life of believers will correspond. As in the life of the church the Spirit is known and honored, the need of a spiritual

ministry will be felt. As the ministry becomes more deeply spiritual, the tone of the church will be raised. The two interact with each other. But how humbling the thought that an earnest, intellectual, eloquent ministry is not necessarily a ministry of the Spirit!

3. Let us make every ministry a matter of unceasing prayer. Let us remember how much the church depends upon it. Let us plead with God for a ministry of the Spirit. When this becomes the desire of the church, the Spirit will not be withheld.

4. What will be the sign of a ministry of the Spirit? There will be a sense of the supernatural, a holy fear of God's presence resting on individuals, and the unmistakable evidence of the presence of God.

The Spirit
and the Flesh

*Are ye so foolish? Having begun in the Spirit, are you
now being made perfect by the flesh?*

Galatians 3:3

*For we are the circumcision, who worship God in the Spirit,
rejoice in Christ Jesus, and have no confidence in the flesh,
though I also might have confidence in the flesh. If anyone
else thinks he may have confidence in the flesh, I more so.*

Philippians 3:3–4

The flesh is the name by which Scripture indicates our
fallen nature—soul and body. The soul at creation was
placed between the spiritual or divine and the sensible or
worldly, to give to each its due, and guide them into that
perfect union that would result in man's attaining his destiny—a spiritual body. When the soul yielded to the temptation of the sensible, it broke away from the rule of the
Spirit and came under the power of the body—it became

flesh. And now the flesh is not only without the Spirit, but even hostile to it: "The flesh lusts against the Spirit" (Galatians 5:17).

In this antagonism of the flesh to the Spirit there are two sides. On the one hand, the flesh lusts against the Spirit in its committing sin and transgressing God's law. On the other hand, its hostility to the Spirit is no less manifested in its seeking to serve God and do His will. In yielding to the flesh, the soul sought itself instead of the God to whom the Spirit linked it; selfishness prevailed over God's will; selfishness became its ruling principle. And now, so subtle and strong is this spirit of self that the flesh, not only in sinning against God but also when the soul seeks to serve God, still asserts its power. It refuses to let the Spirit alone lead, and in its efforts to be "religious" is still the great enemy that hinders and quenches the Spirit. It is because of this deceitfulness of the flesh that there often takes place what Paul speaks of to the Galatians: "Having begun in the Spirit, are you now being made perfect in the flesh?" Unless the surrender to the Spirit is complete, and the waiting upon Him is continued in dependence and humility, what has begun in the Spirit very quickly becomes confidence in the flesh.

And the remarkable thing is that what at first might appear to be a paradox, as soon as the flesh seeks to serve God, it becomes the strength of sin. We know how the Pharisees, with their self-righteousness and carnal religion, fell into pride and selfishness and became the servants of sin. And Paul asked the Galatians the question about perfecting in the flesh what was begun in the Spirit, warning them against the righteousness of works, because the works of the flesh were so manifest that they were in danger of devouring one another. Satan has no more crafty device for keeping souls in bondage than inciting them to practice religion in the flesh. He knows that the power of the flesh can never please God or conquer sin, and that in due time the flesh that has gained supremacy over the Spirit in the service of God will assert and maintain that same supremacy in the service of sin. It is only where the Spirit has the lead and rule in the life of worship that it will have the power to lead and rule in the life of practical obedience. If I am to deny self in my relationships with others, conquer selfishness and temper and lack of love, I must first learn to deny self in my relationship with God. There the soul, the seat of self, must learn to bow to the spirit, where God dwells.

The contrast between the worship in the Spirit and worship in the flesh is beautifully expressed in Paul's description of true circumcision—the circumcision of the heart—whose praise is not of men but of God: "Who worship God in the Spirit, rejoice in Christ Jesus, and have no confidence in the flesh." Placing the rejoicing in Christ Jesus in the center of the verse, as the essence of the Christian faith and life, he calls attention on the one hand to the great danger that besets it, and on the other, the safeguard by which its full enjoyment is secured. Confidence in the flesh is the one thing above all else that renders rejoicing in Christ Jesus ineffective, and worship in the Spirit the one thing that alone makes it life and truth. May the Spirit reveal to us what it means to rejoice in Christ Jesus!

There is a rejoicing in Christ Jesus accompanied by confidence in the flesh that history and experience both teach us. Among the Galatians, the teachers whom Paul opposed so strongly were all preachers of Christ and His cross. But they preached it not as men taught by the Spirit to know the infinite and all-pervading influence of the cross, but as those who having had God's Spirit at the outset, allowed their own wisdom and thoughts to interpret what the cross meant, and so reconciled it with a religion that to a large extent was purely legal and thus carnal. The story of the Galatian church is repeated to this day even in churches that are confident they are free from the Galatian error. Notice how often the doctrine of justification by faith is spoken of as if it were the chief teaching of the epistle, and the doctrine of the Holy Spirit's indwelling and our walking by the Spirit is hardly mentioned.

Christ crucified is the wisdom of God. Confidence in the flesh, in connection with rejoicing in Christ, is confidence in one's own wisdom. Scripture is usually studied, preached, and received in the power of the natural mind, with little emphasis on the need of the Spirit's teaching. It is understood in the confidence with which men know any truth—they know it by human not divine teaching—and in the absence of the receptivity that waits for God to reveal His truth.

Christ, through the Holy Spirit, is not only the wisdom but the power of God. Confidence in the flesh and rejoicing in Christ Jesus is seen and felt in much of the work of the Christian church in which human effort and planning take a larger place than waiting on the power that comes from above. In the larger ecclesiastical organizations, in individual churches, and in the inner life of the spirit and prayer, we see how much unsuccessful effort and repeated failure can be traced to this error. There is no lack of acknowledging Christ as our only hope, and no lack of giving Him the praise that is due Him, and yet so much confidence in the flesh renders it all ineffective.

Let me ask again whether there are not many of you who are seeking a life of full consecration and blessing who find what we have mentioned here to be the secret of your failure. To help those of you who are finding this to be true is one of my first objectives in writing this book. When in a message, conversation, or private prayer, the fullness of Jesus was opened up to you with the possibility of a holy life, your soul felt it was all so beautiful and simple that nothing could hold you back. And perhaps as you accepted what was seen to be so sure and accessible, you entered into a joy and a power before unknown to you. But it did not last. Something was wrong at its root. Your search for the cause was in vain. The reason you were given may have been either that your surrender was incomplete or your faith was not genuine. And yet your soul felt sure that it was ready to give up all and trust Jesus for everything. Your soul could almost despair of an impossible perfection—if perfect consecration and perfect faith were the condition of the blessing. And the promise had been that it would all be so simple—the perfect life for the poor and the weak.

Listen to the teaching of God's Word today: It was confidence in the flesh that spoiled your rejoicing in Christ Jesus. It was self doing what the Spirit alone can do; it was the soul taking the lead in the hope that the Spirit would second its efforts, instead of trusting the Holy Spirit to do all and then waiting on Him. You followed Jesus without denying self. Look again at our text: Paul tells us of the only safeguard against this danger: "We are the circumcision, who worship God in the Spirit, rejoice in Christ Jesus, and have no confidence in the flesh." Here are the two elements of spiritual worship: The Spirit exalts Jesus and abases the flesh. If we would truly rejoice in Jesus and have Him glorified in us; if we would know the glory of Jesus in personal experience, free from the ineffectiveness that marks the efforts of the flesh, we must learn what worship of God by the Spirit is.

I can only repeat that it is the purpose of this book to set forth as God's truth from His blessed Word: Rejoice in Christ Jesus by His Spirit. Rejoice in Him as the glorified one who baptizes with the Holy Spirit. In simplicity and rest, believe that He has given you His own Spirit to live within you. Believe in the gift. Accept it as the secret of the life of Christ in you. Meditate on it, believe His Word concerning it, until your soul bows in awe before God at the glorious truth: The Holy Spirit of God dwells in me.

Yield to His leading, which we have learned is not only in the mind or thoughts but also in the life and disposition. Yield yourself to God to be guided by the Holy Spirit in all your conduct. He is promised to those who love Jesus and obey Him. Remember what the one primary object of His coming was: to restore the departed Lord Jesus to His disciples. "I will not leave you orphans," said Jesus; "I will come again to you." You cannot rejoice in a distant Jesus from whom you are separated. When you try to do it, it takes great effort—you must have the help of the flesh to do it. You can only truly rejoice in a Savior who is present, whom the Holy Spirit reveals within you. As He does this, the flesh is put down; the deeds of the flesh are put to death. Your whole practice of faith must be: I have no confidence in the flesh. I rejoice in Christ Jesus. I worship God in the Spirit.

Beloved believer, having begun in the Spirit, you must continue in the Spirit. Beware of trying to perfect the work of the Spirit in the flesh. Let "no confidence in the flesh" be your battle cry; allow a deep distrust of the flesh and fear of grieving the Spirit by walking after the flesh keep you humble before God. Pray to God for the Spirit of revelation that you may see Jesus as your all and how by the Holy Spirit the divine life takes the place of your life, and Jesus is enthroned as the keeper and guide of your soul.

Blessed God and Father, we thank you for the wondrous provision you have made for your children to draw nigh to you, rejoicing in Christ Jesus, and worshiping you through the Spirit. Grant, we pray, that such may be our life and our Christian service.

We ask you to show us clearly how the great hindrance to such a life is confidence in the flesh. Open our eyes to this snare of Satan. May we all see how secret and subtle is the temptation and how easily we are led to perfect in the flesh what was begun in the Spirit. May we learn to trust you to work in us by your Holy Spirit both to will and to do of your good pleasure.

Teach us, too, we pray, to know how the flesh can be conquered and its power broken. Through the death of your beloved Son our old nature has been crucified. May we count all things but loss, to be made conformable to your death, and to know the power of a life guided by your Holy Spirit. Amen.

Summary

1. Christ is the wisdom and the power of God. The root of all trust in our own strength and wisdom is the idea that we know how to serve God because we have His Word and this is enough. This wisdom of man accepting God's Word is the greatest danger of the church because it is a hidden, subtle form by which we are led to perfect in the flesh what was begun in the Spirit.

2. Our only safety here is the Holy Spirit: a willingness to be taught by Him, a fear of walking after the flesh in the smallest thing, a loving surrender in everything to the obedience of Christ. We need a living faith in the Spirit to possess our life and live through us.

3. Let us realize that there are two motivating principles of life. In most Christians there is a mixed life, yielding to one and then the other. But God's will is that we do not for a moment walk after the flesh, but after the Spirit. The Holy Spirit has been given to bring our life into conformity with God's will. May God show us how the Holy Spirit can help us put to death the life of the flesh and become our new life, revealing Christ in us. Then we can say, "It is no longer I who live, but Christ lives in me" (Galatians 2:20).

4. The church must learn from this epistle that justification by faith is only the means to an end, the entrance to a life of walking by the Spirit of God. We must return to the preaching of John the Baptist: Christ bears the sin of the world; Christ baptizes with the Holy Spirit.

Chapter 27

The Promise of the
Spirit Through Faith

*Christ has redeemed us from the curse of the law, having
become a curse for us (for it is written, "Cursed is
everyone who hangs on a tree"), that the blessing of
Abraham might come upon the Gentiles in
Christ Jesus, that we might receive
the promise of the Spirit through faith.*

Galatians 3:13–14

The word *faith* is used the first time in Scripture in connection with Abraham. His highest praise, the secret of his strength for obedience, and what made him so pleasing to God was that he *believed* God; and so he became the father of all those who believe and the great example of the blessing that divine favor bestows and the path by which it comes. Just as God proved himself to Abraham as the God who quickens the dead, He does to us in a fuller measure by giving His Spirit to dwell in us. And just as this life-giving power came to Abraham through faith, so the promise of the Spirit is made ours by faith. All the lessons of Abraham's life centered in this: We receive the promise of the Spirit through faith. If we want to know the faith by which the Spirit is received, how it comes and how it grows, we can study Abraham's story.

In Abraham's life story is the illustration of what faith is: the spiritual sense by which a person recognizes and accepts the revelation of God and a spiritual consciousness awakened by that revelation. It was because God chose Abraham and determined to reveal himself through him that Abraham became a man of faith. Each new revelation was an act of the divine will; it is through that will and the revelation by which it carries out its purpose that faith is born. The more distinct the revelation, the deeper faith is stirred in the soul. Paul speaks of "trust in the living God": It is only as the life-giving power of the divine life draws nigh and touches the soul that a living faith is called forth. Faith is not an independent act by which, in our own strength, we take what God says. Nor is it an entirely passive state in which we allow God to do with us what He will. Rather, it is that receptivity of soul in which as God draws near and as His living power speaks to us and touches us, we yield ourselves to Him and accept His word and working in us.

It is evident then, that faith deals with two things: the presence of the Lord and the word of the Lord. It is His living presence that reveals His word in power. It is because of this vital connection that we see so much reading and preaching of the Word of God bearing little fruit, so much striving and praying for faith with so little result. Many use the Word of God without the presence of the living God.

Faith has been defined as taking God at His word. To many this means taking the word as God's; they miss the power of taking *God* at His word. A key has no value until I use it in the lock of the door I want to open. So it is only in direct and living contact with God himself that the Word opens my heart to believe. Faith takes *God* at His word. I may have God's Book and all His precious promises clear and full; I may have learned perfectly how to trust in the promises to see them fulfilled, and yet utterly fail to find the longed-for blessing. The faith that enters into the inheritance is the attitude of soul that waits for God himself, first to speak His word, and then to do what He has spoken. Faith is fellowship with God; faith is surrender to God, the impression made by His drawing nigh, the possession He takes of the soul by His word, holding and preparing it for His work. When once the soul has been awakened, it watches for every appearance of the divine will; it listens for and accepts every indication of the divine presence; it looks for and expects the fulfillment of every divine promise.

Such was the faith through which Abraham inherited the promises. Such is the faith by which the blessing of Abraham comes upon the Gentiles and by which we receive the promise of the Spirit. In our study of the work of the Holy Spirit and of the way in which He comes, let us hold on to this word: "We receive the promise of the Spirit by faith." Whether seeking to know the full consciousness of the Spirit's indwelling, a deeper assurance of God's love in the heart, a greater manifestation of His fruit, a clearer experience of His guiding into all truth, or for the endue-ment of power to do His work, let us remember that the law of faith on which grace is grounded demands its fullest application: "According to your faith let it be to you" (Matthew 9:29). We receive the promise of the Spirit by faith. Let us seek for Abraham's blessing in Abraham's faith.

Let our faith begin where his began: in meeting God and waiting on God. The Lord appeared unto Abraham. And he fell on his face, and God talked with him. Let us also look to our God to do this wonderful thing for us: to talk with us, and also to fill us with His Holy Spirit. "Those who are of faith are blessed with believing Abraham" (Galatians 3:9). To Abraham, both when his own body was "as dead," and later on, when his son was bound on the altar, ready to be sacrificed, He came as the life-giving God. Abraham believed God, who quickens the dead. He offered Isaac, counting on God to raise him up, if necessary. To us He comes, offering to fill us spirit, soul, and body with the power of a divine life through His Holy Spirit. May we be like Abraham: When he looked at the promise of God, he did not waver in unbelief, but was strong through faith, giving glory to God, being assured that what He promised He was able to accomplish. Let us be filled with the faith of Him who promised, our hearts focused on Him who is able to accomplish it. It is faith in God that opens our heart and prepares us to submit to Him and to receive His divine work in us. God waits on us to fill us with His Spirit. It is God alone who will do it. To read about it and meditate on it, to long for it, even to consecrate ourselves and grasp the truth that the Spirit wants to dwell within us—all this has its place, but does not bring the blessing. We need a heart of faith in the living God and in that faith to abide in Him, wait on Him, and worship Him. In close fellowship with

God, the answer will come; the Holy Spirit will be given in full measure.

Taking a position of faith, we must remain in it. We have the Spirit, let us now be filled with Him. As we think of some manifestation of the Spirit by which a need was revealed, or go to the Word to be led into the will of God concerning our life in the Spirit, we shall be kept in that sense of dependence out of which childlike trust is formed and nurtured. We will be preserved from a life of stress and strife, so often leading to failure, because in the very attempt to serve God in the Spirit, we still have confidence in the flesh because of something we did, or thought we did. The underpinning of our life—whether meditating on the Word, in silent prayer or public worship, in service to God or man—will be the assurance that supersedes every other: The Holy Spirit and His guidance and inspiration belong to those who ask.

Such faith will not be without trials. One day we will know the Spirit's leading and another day feel as though He is far from us. This is when we must learn that a living faith rejoices in a living God—even when feelings contradict. The life of Christ was given to us through His death and resurrection and fills an empty vessel. We receive the promise of the Spirit through faith. As our faith grows, the Spirit's presence will be fuller and deeper. Each new revelation of God to Abraham made his faith stronger and his acquaintance with God more intimate. When God drew near, he knew what to expect; he could trust Him even in the most trying times—even when asked to offer his only son as a sacrifice. It is the faith that waits every day on the living God, the faith that in ever-increasing readiness yields to Him that receives the promise of the Spirit.

It was in God's presence that faith was awakened and strengthened in Abraham and other saints of the Old Testament. It was in Jesus' presence on earth that unbelief was cast out, and that weak faith became strong. It was in the presence of the glorified One that faith received the blessing of Pentecost. The throne of God is opened to us in Christ; it is the throne of God and the Lamb: As we wait in humble worship and walk in loving service before the throne, the river of the water of life that flows under it will flow into us, and through us, and out to others.

Blessed God, who by your divine love and power reveal yourself to each of your children, increase within us, we pray, the faith through which alone we can know you. Whether you come as the Almighty, the Redeemer, or the indwelling Spirit, it is faith you seek, and according to faith we receive. O Father, convince us that we have just as much of the Spirit as we have faith!

It is your presence that awakens faith in the soul yielded to you. Draw us into your holy presence and keep us there. Deliver us from the fascination of the world and the flesh so that your glory may be our all-consuming desire. We long to take your words and allow them to dwell richly in us. We want a stillness of soul before you, to trust and believe that you have given us your Spirit. Let us live the life of faith, believing in the work of your Holy Spirit. Amen.

Summary

1. Faith is the one thing that pleases God. In all worship and work that is acceptable to God in Christ Jesus, it is

faith that receives the testimony that we are well-pleasing to Him. This is because faith goes beyond self, gives God alone the glory, looks only to the Son, and is receptive to the Spirit. Faith is not merely the positive conviction that God's Word or promise is true; there may be this confidence even in the power of the flesh. Faith is the spiritual organ of the soul through which it waits on the living God, listens to Him, takes His words, has communion with Him. It is as this habit of soul is cultivated, as we live our whole life by faith, that the Spirit can enter fully and flow freely to others.

2. The Spirit is called the incorruptible seed (1 Peter 1:23) because He is cast into the soul with the Word. The Word is the material seed, but the Spirit is the virtual seed.

3. You long for the power of the Holy Spirit to keep you looking to Jesus, to reveal Jesus as the ever-present Savior from sin. Begin each day with a quiet act of meditation and faith. In confidence turn inwardly, not to see the work the Holy Spirit does, but to yield your spirit to Him who dwells in secret. Say with humility: "I have within me, small and hidden, the seed of the kingdom, the seed of eternal life. I have found the seed of the living word, the seed of God, within me." Bow before God in holy fear because He works in you, and let faith take time before Him to become confident and conscious of the fact that the Holy Spirit is within you.

4. His seed abides in us to keep us from sin. Go out into daily life in the strength of the faith that the Holy Spirit dwells within and that the Father will grant that He works effectually to keep you from sin. Pause frequently

in self-reflection, allowing the Spirit to remind you that you are God's temple.

5. As individual believers enter into this life of faith and walk in it, there will be power to pray for the Spirit to come in power upon all flesh.

Chapter 28

Walking by the Spirit

*I say then: Walk in the Spirit, and you shall not fulfill the
lust of the flesh. And those who are Christ's have crucified
the flesh with its passions and desires. If we live
in the Spirit, let us also walk in the Spirit.*

Galatians 5:16, 24–25

"If we live in the Spirit, let us also walk in the Spirit." These
words suggest to us clearly the difference between the carnal and the spiritual Christian life. In the former the Christian may be content to live in the Spirit, in the sense that
he has the Spirit by virtue of his salvation; he is satisfied
with knowing that he has the new life, but he does not *walk
in the Spirit.* The spiritual follower, on the contrary, is not
content unless his whole walk and conversation is in the
power of the Spirit. He walks by the Spirit and so does not
fulfill the lusts of the flesh because he is filled with the
Spirit.

As the Christian strives to walk worthily of God and be
well-pleasing to Him in all things, he is often deeply trou-
bled by the still-evident power of sin, and seeks the cause

for which he so often fails to conquer it. He usually feels that it is due to his lack of faith or faithfulness, his natural weakness, or the power of Satan. But he must not rest content with this solution. It would be better to press on to find the deeper reason why all these things, from which Christ secured deliverance, can still overcome us. One of the deepest secrets of the Christian life is the knowledge that the power that keeps the Spirit of God from ruling is our own flesh. He who knows what the flesh is and how it works and how it must be dealt with, will be the overcomer.

We know that it was because of their ignorance of this fact that the Galatians so miserably failed. It was this that led them to attempt to perfect in the flesh what was begun in the Spirit (Galatians 3:3). It was this that made them prey to those who desired "to make a good showing in the flesh" that "they may boast in your flesh" (Galatians 6:12–13). They didn't know how incorrigibly corrupt the flesh was. They didn't know that, as sinful as our nature is when fulfilling its own lusts, as sinful as it is when making "a good showing in the flesh," it can yield itself to the service of God and attempt to perfect what the Spirit began. Because the Galatians were not aware of this possibility, they were unable to check the flesh in its passions and lusts; these obtained the victory over them, so that they did what they did not wish to do. They didn't know that as long as the flesh, self-effort, and self-will had any influence in serving God, it would remain strong to serve sin, and that the only way to render it ineffective to do evil was to render it ineffective in its attempts to do good!

It is to discover the truth of God concerning the flesh, both in its service to God and to sin, that this epistle was written. Paul wanted to teach them that the Spirit alone is the power of the Christian life, and that this power cannot be effective unless the flesh is utterly denied and set aside. In answer to the question of how this can be, he gives the wonderful answer that is one of the central thoughts of God's revelation. The crucifixion and death of Christ is the revelation not only of atonement for sin but also of power that frees from the dominion of sin as it is rooted in the flesh. When Paul in the midst of his teaching about the walk in the Spirit tells us, "And those who are Christ's have crucified the flesh with its passions and desires" (Galatians 5:24), he is telling us the only way by which deliverance from the flesh is found. To understand these words, "crucified the flesh," and experience it, is the secret of walking not after the flesh but after the Spirit. Let each one who longs to walk by the Spirit seek to grasp its meaning.

In Scripture, "the flesh" means the whole of our human nature in its present condition under the power of sin. It includes our whole being—spirit, soul, and body. After the fall, God said of man, "he is indeed flesh" (Genesis 6:3). All his powers, intellect, emotions, and will are under the power of the flesh. Scripture speaks of the will of the flesh, of the mind of the flesh, of the passions and lusts of the flesh. It tells us that in our flesh no good dwells. The mind of the flesh is at enmity against God. On this ground it teaches that nothing that is of the flesh, nothing that the fleshly mind or will thinks or does, however fair the show it makes, and however much men may glory in it, can have any value in the sight of God. It warns us that our greatest danger in our Christian walk, the cause of our weakness and failure, is our having confidence in the flesh, its wisdom and its work. It tells us that to be pleasing to God, this flesh, with its self-will and self-effort, must be entirely given up in order to make way for the will and work of another, the Spirit of God. The only way to be made free from the power of the flesh is to crucify it.

"Those who are Christ's *have crucified the flesh*." The tendency is to speak of crucifying the flesh as a thing that has to be done. Scripture speaks of it as something that has already been done: "Our old man was crucified with Him, that the body of sin might be done away with, that we should no longer be slaves of sin" (Romans 6:6). "I have been crucified with Christ; it is no longer I who live, but Christ lives in me" (Galatians 2:20). Those who are Christ's *have crucified the flesh*. This is a fact accomplished on the cross of our Lord Jesus Christ. Through it the world has been crucified unto me and I unto the world. What Christ did through the eternal Spirit on the cross, He did not as an individual, but in the name of human nature, which, as its Head, He had taken upon himself. Everyone who accepts Christ receives Him as the crucified one—not only the merit, but the power of His crucifixion—and is united and identified with Him. They that are of Christ Jesus have, by virtue of their accepting the crucified Christ as their life, given up their flesh to the cross.

Some still ask, "What does it mean to have *crucified* the flesh?" Some are content with the general truth that the cross takes away the curse that was upon all flesh. Others think they must cause the flesh pain and suffering; they must deny it and mortify it. Others think of the moral influence the thought of the cross will impart. In each of these views there is an element of truth. But if they are to be realized in power, we must go to the root thought: To crucify the flesh is to give it over to the curse. The cross and the curse are inseparable (Deuteronomy 21:23; Galatians 3:13). To say "Our old man has been crucified with him, I have been crucified with Christ" is a very serious declaration. It means I confess that my old nature, my self, deserves the curse and that there is no way of ridding myself of it but by death. I voluntarily give it over to death. I have accepted as my life the Christ who came to give himself, His flesh, to the cursed death of the cross—who received His new life only because of that death and by virtue of it. I give my old man, my flesh, self, with its will and work, as a sinful, accursed thing, to the cross. It is nailed there. In Christ I am dead to it and free from it.

The power of this truth depends upon its being known, accepted, and acted upon. If I only know the cross for its substitution, but not as Paul gloried in it—in its fellowship (Galatians 6:14), I can never experience its power to sanctify. As the blessed truth of its fellowship dawns upon me, I see how by faith I can enter into and live in spiritual communion with Jesus who, as my head and leader, made and proved the cross the only way to the throne. This spiritual union, maintained by faith, becomes a moral one. I have the same mind or disposition that was in Christ Jesus. I regard the flesh as sinful and only fit for the curse. I accept the cross with its death to what is flesh, secured to me in Jesus, as the only way to become free from the power of self and to walk in newness of life by the Spirit.

The way that faith in the power of the cross is a revelation and at the same time the removal of the curse and the power of the flesh is a very simple truth and yet a profound one. I begin to understand that in living by the Spirit there is the danger of yielding to the flesh or self in my attempt to serve God. This renders the cross of Christ ineffective (1 Corinthians 1:17; Galatians 3:3; 5:12–13; Philippians 3:3–4; Colossians 2:18–23). I see now how all that was of man and nature, of law and human effort, was forever judged by God on Calvary. There flesh proved that with all its wisdom and all its "religion" it hated and rejected the Son of God. There God proved that the only way to be delivered from the flesh is to put it to death as an accursed thing. I begin to understand that I need to look upon the flesh as God does; to accept the death-warrant that the cross brings to everything in me that is of the flesh; to look upon it and all that comes from it as a thing cursed. As this habit of soul grows on me, I learn to fear nothing so much as myself. I tremble at the thought of allowing the flesh, my natural mind and will, to usurp the place of the Holy Spirit! My whole attitude toward Christ is that of humble fear in the consciousness of having within me that accursed thing that is always ready, as an angel of light, to intrude itself in the holiest of all and lead me astray to serve God not in the Spirit of Christ but in the power of the flesh. It is in such a humble fear that the believer is taught to believe fully in the need, but also the provision, of the Holy Spirit to entirely take the place that the flesh once had and day by day to glory in the cross, of which he can say, "By it I have been crucified to the world."

We often look for the cause of failure in the Christian life. We think that because we are sound on what the Galatians did not understand—justification by faith alone—their danger cannot be ours. Oh, that we knew to what an extent we have allowed the flesh to work in our Christian walk! Let us pray God for grace to know it as our bitterest enemy, and the enemy of Christ. Free grace does not only mean the pardon of sin, it means the power of a new life through the Holy Spirit. Let us consent to what God says of the flesh and all that comes of it: that it is sinful, condemned, cursed. Let us fear nothing so much as the hidden workings of our own flesh. Let us accept the teaching of God's Word: "For I know that in me (that is, in my flesh) nothing good dwells; for to will is present with me, but how to perform what is good I do not find" (Romans 7:18). Let us ask God to show us to what extent the Spirit must possess us if we are to be pleasing to Him in all things. Let us believe that as we daily glory in the cross, and in prayer and obedience yield the flesh to the death of the cross, Christ will accept our surrender and by His divine power maintain in us the life of the Spirit. We shall learn not only to live by the Spirit, but as those made free from the power of the flesh our walk by the Spirit in our daily lives.

Dearest God, I beseech you to reveal to me the full meaning of what your Word has been teaching me, that it is as one who has crucified the flesh with its passions and lusts that I can walk by the Spirit.

Teach me, Father, to see that all that is of nature and of self is of the flesh, that the flesh has been tested by you and found wanting, worthy of nothing but the curse and death. Teach me that my Lord Jesus led the way and acknowledged the justice of this curse, that I too might be willing and have the strength to give it up to the cross as an accursed thing. Give me grace day by day, lest I allow the flesh to intrude upon the work of the Spirit and to grieve Him. And teach me that the Holy Spirit has been given to be the life of my life and to fill my whole being with the power of the death and life of my blessed Lord.

Lord Jesus, who sent your Holy Spirit to secure the uninterrupted enjoyment of your presence and your saving power within us, I yield myself to be entirely yours, to live wholly and only under His leading. I do with my whole heart desire to regard the flesh as crucified and accursed. I solemnly consent to live as one who has been crucified. Savior, you have accepted my surrender; I trust in you to keep me this day walking by the Spirit. Amen.

Summary

1. The power of Christ's life cannot work in me apart from the power of His death. His death alone deals effectually with the flesh, with self, with the natural life, to make way for the new life of the Holy Spirit. We must pray to see how entirely the flesh must die, how actually and entirely the Holy Spirit must cast out our self-life if He is to reveal in us the Christ-life.

2. Many will say that calling the flesh, the natural man, the life of self, an accursed thing is a hard saying. It is easy to encircle the cross with flowers and say a thousand beautiful things about it. But what God says of it is this: The cross is a curse. The Son of God on the cross "was made a curse." If my flesh is crucified, it can only be because it is accursed. It is a blessed moment in life when a person understands what a cursed thing sin is. It is still more blessed, and may work a deeper humiliation, when God shows someone how he has cherished the

flesh, and for its sake grieved the Holy Spirit of God.

3. The flesh and the Spirit are the two powers. Under the rule of one or the other every act is done. Let our steps be after the Spirit.

4. The death of Christ led to glory, where He received and gave the Holy Spirit. It is a life where death to the flesh is the ruling principle in which the power of the Spirit can be revealed.

5. The church, walking in the fear of the Lord and in the comfort of the Holy Spirit, was multiplied. A deep, humble fear of the holy presence within, a fear of listening to self instead of Him, is one secret of walking in the comfort of the Holy Spirit.

Chapter 29

The Spirit of Love

But the fruit of the Spirit is love.

Galatians 5:22

Now I beg you, brethren, through the Lord Jesus Christ, and through the love of the Spirit, that you strive together with me in prayers to God for me.

Romans 15:30

. . . who also declared to us your love in the Spirit.

Colossians 1:8

Our subject in this chapter leads us into the very center of the inner sanctuary. We are speaking of the love of the Spirit. We will learn that love is not only the fruit of the Spirit from which all others come, but the Spirit is nothing less than divine love itself come down to dwell in us, and *we have only as much of the Spirit as we have of love.*

God is a Spirit: God is love. In these two words we have the only attempt that Scripture makes to give us, in human language, what may be called a definition of God. (The third expression of the same sort—God is light—is a figurative one.) As a Spirit, He has life in himself, is independent of all around Him, and has power over all to enter into it, to penetrate it with His own life, to communicate himself to it. It is through the Spirit that God is the Father of spirits, that He is the God of creation, the God and redeemer of man. Everything owes its life to the Spirit of God. And this is so because God is love. Within himself He is love, as seen in the Father giving all He has to the Son, and the Son seeking all He has in the Father. In this life of love between the Father and the Son, the Spirit is the bond of fellowship. The Father is the loving one, the fountain; the Son, the beloved one, the great reservoir of love, always receiving and always giving back; and the Spirit is the living love that makes them one. In Him the divine life of love has its unceasing flow, even to overflowing. The same love with which the Father loves the Son can be ours. It is through the Spirit that this love of God is revealed and communicated to us. It was the Spirit who led Jesus in His work of love for which He was anointed—to preach glad tidings to the poor and deliverance to the captives. In the love and power of that same Spirit, Jesus offered himself as a sacrifice for us. The Spirit comes to lavish us with the love of God. The Spirit *is* the love of God.

When the Holy Spirit enters us, His first task is to shed abroad in our hearts the love of God. What He gives is not only the faith or the experience of how greatly God loves us, but something infinitely more glorious. The love of God enters our hearts as a spiritual existence, a living power. The outpouring of the Spirit is the inpouring of love. This love possesses our hearts—the same love with which God loves all His children; the love that overflows to all the world is within us. The Spirit is the life of the love of God; the Spirit in us is the love of God taking up residence within us.

Such is the relationship between the Spirit and the love of God. Now let us consider the relationship between our spirit and love. We must here again refer to what has been said of man's threefold nature: body, soul, and spirit—established in creation and disrupted by the fall. We have seen how the soul, as the seat of self-consciousness, was to be subject to the spirit, the seat of God-consciousness. Sin is simply self-assertion—the soul refusing the rule of the spirit in order to gratify itself in the lust of the body. The fruit of sin is that self ascended the throne of the soul to rule there instead of God. Selfishness became the ruling power in man's life. The self that refused God His right, at the same time refused others their due, and the awful story of sin in the world is simply the history of the origin, growth, power, and reign of self. It is only when the original order is restored, when the soul gives the spirit precedence, that selfishness will be conquered and love for others will flow from our love for God. In other words, as the renewed spirit becomes the residence of the Spirit of God, and as the regenerate man yields to the Spirit's control, love will again become the motivation of his life. To every disciple the Master says, "If anyone desires to come after Me, let him deny himself, and take up his cross, and follow Me" (Matthew 16:24). Many have sought in vain to follow Jesus, but could not because they have neglected what is indispensable—self-denial. Self cannot follow Jesus because it cannot love as He loves.

If we understand this, we are prepared to admit the claim that Jesus makes, *and that the world makes,* that the proof of discipleship is *love.* The change we have undergone is so divine, the deliverance from the power of self and sin so complete, the fulfilling of the law—love—ought to be the natural outflow of the new life of every believer. If this is not so, it is only proof of how little we understand our calling to walk after the Spirit. Displays of selfishness, flaring tempers, harsh judgments, unkind words, lack of patience and gentleness are simply proof that we do not yet understand what it means to be full of the Spirit of Christ. We are still carnal and not spiritual.

It was so with the Corinthians. In them we see the remarkable phenomenon of a church enriched in everything by Him in all utterance and all knowledge, even as the testimony of Christ was confirmed in them, so that they came short in no gift, and yet were so obviously lacking in love. (See 1 Corinthians 1:5–7). The sad spectacle teaches us how, under the first moving of the Holy Spirit, the natural powers of the soul may be greatly affected without the self being fully surrendered. Thus, fruit of the Spirit may be seen even while love is still lacking. It shows that it is not enough for the Spirit to take hold of these soul-endowments and stir them to action. Something more is needed. He has entered the soul that through it He may obtain a firm and undivided influence in both the soul and the spirit—that self being deposed, God may reign. The sign that self is deposed and that God reigns will be love.

The state of the Galatians was not very different, to whom the words "The fruit of the Spirit is love" were addressed. Though their error was not that of the Corinthians—boasting of gifts and knowledge but trusting in carnal observances and ordinances—the result in both was the same: The Spirit's full dominion was not allowed, and so the flesh ruled in them, causing bitterness, envy, and enmity. Even today the rule of the flesh is still found in much of what bears the name of the Christian church. On the one hand, there is trust in gifts and knowledge, sound creed and earnest work; on the other hand, satisfaction in forms and services leaves the flesh in full vigor, and so the Spirit is not free to work. A church or a Christian professing to have the Holy Spirit must prove it in the exhibition of a Christlike love.

We have the love of God within our reach; it is dwelling within us. Since the day when, by believing, we were sealed with the Holy Spirit, the love of God has been shed abroad in our hearts. Though there may be small manifestations of it seen in our lives, and though we may not always feel it, it is there. The love of God has come into our hearts by the Holy Spirit; the two cannot be separated. If we would come now to the experience of the blessing, we must begin by a very simple faith in what the Word says. The Word is Spirit-breathed, the divinely prepared vehicle through which the Spirit reveals who He is and what He does. As we take the Word as divine truth, the Spirit will make it truth in us. Let us confirm that the Holy Spirit, bearer to us of God's love, has been in our hearts ever since we became God's children. If the veil of the flesh has not been rent in us, the outpouring and power of that love will have been weak and hidden from our consciousness. Let us believe that He dwells within us to reveal the love of God.

In the faith that the Spirit of love is within us, let us

look to the Father in earnest prayer to plead for His working in our inner being, that we may be rooted and
grounded in love. As the answer comes, the Spirit will
reveal to us the love of God—the love of the Father to
Christ, the love of Christ to us. Through the same Spirit
this love returns to its source as our love to God and to
Christ. Because the Spirit reveals the same love to all God's
children, our experience of it coming from God or returning to God is equal with our love to the brethren. Like rain
descending from heaven, flowing to springs and streams,
and rising to heaven again, so is the love of God—His love
to us, our love to Him, and our love to our brethren. The
love of God is within you by the Holy Spirit. Believe it,
rejoice in it, and prove that the Spirit of God is the love of
God.

*Blessed Lord Jesus, I bow before you as Love incarnate.
The Father's love gave you to us. Your coming was a mission
of love. Your whole life was love, your death its divine seal.
The new commandment you gave your disciples was love.
Your prayer before the throne is that your disciples may be
one as you are one with the Father, and that His love may be
in them. The primary trait of your likeness that you long to
see in us is love. The irresistible proof to the world of your
divine mission will be the love of your disciples for one
another. And the Spirit that comes from you to us is the Spirit
of your self-sacrificing love, teaching your saints to live and
die for others just as you did.*

*Holy Lord, look upon your church, look upon our hearts.
Wherever you see that love like yours is lacking, deliver your
saints from all that is selfish and unloving. Teach them to*

yield self, which cannot love, to the accursed cross—to await the fate it deserves. Teach us to believe that we can love because the Holy Spirit has been given to us. Teach us to begin to love and serve, to sacrifice self and live for others, that love in action may learn its power, may be increased and perfected. Teach us to believe that because you live in us, your love is in us, too, and we can love as you did. Lord Jesus, love of God, your own Spirit is within us; let Him break through and fill our whole life with love! Amen.

Summary

1. The way whereby the Spirit works any grace in the believer is by stirring them up to act upon it. The Spirit of God does not effectually work love or give strength to love until we act upon it, because all inward graces are discerned by their acts as seed in the ground is by its springing up. We cannot see or feel any such thing as love to God or man in our hearts before we act upon it. We do not know our spiritual strength, except as we use and exercise it.

2. The love of God, the fount from which flows love to men, has been shed abroad in our hearts through the Holy Spirit that was given to us. The love is there, but we may remain ignorant of it unless we begin to believe that we have the power to obey the command and to love God and man with our whole heart. Faith and obedience always precede the conscious enjoyment and experience of the Spirit's power. As God is love to you, show love all around you.

3. Let us now seek to keep the two sides of the truth in harmony. On the one hand, wait often in God's holy

presence for the quickening of your faith and conscious-ness that the loving Holy Spirit dwells in you. On the other hand, give yourself, apart from what you feel, to a wholehearted obedience to the command of love and act out in your life the gentleness and forbearance, kindness and helpfulness, self-sacrifice and benevolence of Christ Jesus. Live in the love of Jesus, and you will be a messen-ger of His love to everyone you meet, to everyone who does not yet know Him. The more intimate your com-munion with Jesus, and the more the life of heaven is given through the Holy Spirit, the more accurate will be your translation of that life into the relationships of your daily life.

4. No man has seen God at any time, but as we love one another, God abides in us. The compensation for not seeing God with our natural eye is this: We have one another to love. If we do this, God abides in us. We don't need to ask if our brother is worthy: God's love to us and to him is love to the unworthy. It is with this love, the divine love, that the Holy Spirit fills us, teaching us to love as He loves.

Chapter 30

The Unity of the Spirit

*I . . . beseech you to walk worthy of the calling with which
you were called, with all lowliness and gentleness, with
longsuffering, bearing with one another in love,
endeavoring to keep the unity of the Spirit in the bond of
peace. There is one body and one Spirit, just as you
were called in one hope of your calling.*

Ephesians 4:1–4

*There are diversities of gifts, but the same Spirit. One and
the same Spirit works all these things, distributing to each
one individually as He wills. For by one Spirit we were all
baptized into one body; whether Jews or Greeks, whether
slaves or free; and have all been made
to drink into one Spirit.*

1 Corinthians 12:4, 11, 13

We know how in the first three chapters of Ephesians, Paul
presents the glory of Christ Jesus as the head of the church
and the glory of God's grace in the church as the body of
Christ indwelt by the Holy Spirit, growing up into a

dwelling of God through the Spirit and destined to be filled with all the fullness of God. Having thus lifted the believer to his life hidden in Christ, Paul comes back down with him to the level of his life on earth, and in the second half of the epistle teaches him how to walk worthy of his calling. The first lesson he gives in regard to this life and walk on earth rests on the foundation truth that the Holy Spirit has united him not only to Christ our head in heaven but also to Christ's body on earth—the church. The Spirit dwells in Christ's body, with each of its members, and the full, healthy ministry of the Spirit can only be found where a right relationship exists between the individual and the whole body. His first concern in his holy walk, therefore, must be to endeavor to maintain the unity of the Spirit. If this unity of the Spirit in the body were fully functioning, the principal virtues of the Christian life would be humility and meekness, in which each would deny himself for the sake of others and uphold one another in love amid differences and shortcomings. So the new commandment would be kept, and the Spirit of Christ—the Spirit of love—sacrificing itself for others, would have the freedom to do His blessed work.

The need of such teaching is remarkably illustrated by the first epistle to the Corinthians. In that church there were abundant operations of the workings of the Holy Spirit. The gifts of the Spirit were strikingly manifested, but the fruits of the Spirit were remarkably absent. They did not understand that there are diversities of gifts, but the same Spirit; that amid differences, one and the same Spirit distributes to each individually as He will; that all had been baptized into one Spirit, into one body, and all made to partake of the same Spirit. They didn't know the better way—that the first fruit of all the fruits of the Spirit is the love that seeks not its own and finds its happiness in serving others.

To each believer who would fully yield himself to the leading of the Spirit as well as to the church as a whole, the *unity of the Spirit* is a truth filled with rich, spiritual blessing. A pastor I knew always said, "Have a deep reverence for the work of the Holy Spirit within you." That injunction needs as its complement a second one: Have a deep reverence for the work of the Holy Spirit in your brother or sister in Christ. This is not an easy thing—even Christians advanced in other respects often fail here. The cause is not hard to see. It has been observed that the faculty of discrimination—the observing of differences—is one of the earliest to be developed in children. The power of cooperation—the observing of harmony amid apparent diversity—is a faculty that appears later. The lesson finds its most striking exemplification in the Christian life and church. We need little help to know where we differ from other Christians or churches, to contend for our views or to judge their errors in doctrine or conduct. But grace is indeed present when, amid conduct that irritates or grieves us or teaching that appears to us unscriptural or offensive, we give place to the Spirit and have faith in the power of love to maintain unity in the face of strife and division.

Keep the unity of the Spirit. This is God's command to every believer. It is the new commandment—to love one another—in a new form, tracing the love back to the Spirit by which it has its life. If you would obey the command, note carefully that it is the unity of *the Spirit*. There is a unity of creed or custom, of church or choice, in which the bond is more of the flesh than of the Spirit. If you would keep the unity of the Spirit, remember the following:

First, know that the Spirit in you is the means by which the unity finds its power of attachment and victory. There is much in you that is of self and of the flesh that can excel in a unity that is of this earth but that will greatly hinder the unity of the Spirit. Confess that it is not by your own strength that you can truly love; all that is of yourself is selfish and does not promote the unity of the Spirit. Be humbled by the thought that it is only God in you that can unite with what appears displeasing to you. Be thankful for the fact that He is in you and that He can conquer self and thereby love even what seems unloving.

Seek to know and appreciate the spirit in your brother, with whom you are to be united. As in you, so also in him, there is but a beginning, a hidden seed of the divine life, surrounded by much that is yet carnal—often trying and displeasing. We need a heart humbled by the fact that we are unworthy, a heart loving and quick to excuse our brother—for so did Jesus on the last night: "The spirit is willing but the flesh is weak." We need to look persistently at what there is in our brother of the image and Spirit of Christ. Esteem him not by what he is in himself, but by what he is in Christ. As you sense how the same life and Spirit that you owe to free grace is in him, too, the unity of the Spirit will triumph over the prejudice and lack of love that is of the flesh. Your spirit acknowledging the spirit of your brother will bind you in the unity of the Spirit that is from above.

Keep this unity of the Spirit active. The bond among the

members of your own physical body is living and real, maintained by the circulation of blood and the life it carries. "In one Spirit we were all baptized into one body. There is one body and one Spirit." The inner union of life must find expression and be strengthened in the manifested communion of love. Endeavor in all your thoughts and judgments of other believers to exercise the love that thinks no evil. Never say an unkind word of a child of God, nor of others for that matter. Love every believer, not because he is in agreement with you or pleasing to you, but for the sake of the Spirit of Christ who is in him. Give yourself particularly to love and labor for God's children within your reach who through ignorance or weakness or waywardness do not know that they have the Spirit or are grieving Him. The work of the Spirit is to build up a habitation for God; yield yourself to the Spirit in you to do this work. Recognize your dependence upon the fellowship of the Spirit in your brother, and his dependence upon you, and seek to grow with him in the unity of love.

Take your part in the united intercession that rises to God for the unity of His church. Take up and continue the intercession of the great High Priest for all who believe so that they may be one. The church is one in the life of Christ and the love of the Spirit. It is not yet one in the manifested unity of the Spirit. Hence the need of the command: Keep the unity. Plead with God for the mighty working of His Spirit in every church and circle of believers. When the tide is low, each small pool along the shore with its inhabitants is separated from the rest by a rocky barrier. As the tide rises, the barriers are flooded over, and all meet in one great ocean. So it will be with the church of Christ. As the Spirit of God comes, according to the promise—as floods upon the dry ground—each will know the power in himself and in others, and self will disappear as the Spirit is known and honored.

How is this wondrous change to be brought about and the time shortened until the prayer is fulfilled: "That they all may be one, as You, Father, are in Me, and I in You; that they also may be one in Us, that the world may believe that You sent Me" (John 17:21)? Let each one begin by looking within. Resolve now that this shall be the mark of your life: to have and to know the indwelling Spirit. If you are to live in harmony with everyone, He must have control of your whole being. Pray that the Father may grant you, according to the riches of His glory, to be strengthened with might by His Spirit in the inner man. Christ's Spirit will be in you the holy anointing, the oil of consecration, to set you apart and equip you to be, as Christ was, a messenger of the Father's love. In the humility of daily life, in the forbearance of love amid differences and difficulties in the church, in the empathy and self-sacrifice that finds and helps those in need, the Spirit in you will prove that He belongs to all the members of the body. Through you His love reaches out to all around you in blessing.

Blessed Lord Jesus, on your last night on earth your prayer for your disciples was "that they also may be one in Us." Your desire was to see them a united flock, gathered and kept in your hand of love. Lord Jesus, now you are on the throne and we come to you with the same plea: Keep us, that we may be one! Pray for us, our great High Priest, that we may be made perfect in one that the world may know that the Father loves us as He loved you.

Lord, thank you for the signs that you are awakening in your church the desire for the manifestation to the world of the unity of your people. Grant, we pray, to this end, the mighty working of your Holy Spirit. May every believer know the Spirit that is in him and that is in his brother, and in all lowliness and love keep the unity of the Spirit with those with whom he comes into contact. May the leaders of your church see the unity of the Spirit as stronger than any human bond. May all who have put on the Lord Jesus, above all else put on love, the bond of perfection.

We ask you to draw your people together in united prayer at your feet, that you might reveal your presence in all. Fill us with your Spirit and we shall be one. Amen.

Summary

1. The health of every member, every function, depends upon the health of the surrounding members. Either the healing power of the sound member must expel what is unhealthy, or the unhealthy member will spread its illness to every part. I am more dependent upon my brother than I realize. He is more dependent on me than he knows. The Spirit I have is the Spirit of Christ, who dwells also in my brother. All I receive is meant for him as well. To keep the unity of the Spirit in active exercise, to live in loving fellowship with believers around me, is the life in the Spirit.

2. That they may be made perfect in one. We approach perfection as we approach unity. Perfection is impossible in a state of separation. My life is not wholly given to

me, but a part of it is given to my brother, to be available to me when I am in fellowship with him.

3. It has taken you time and prayer and faith to know the Spirit of God within you; it will take time and prayer and faith, and much love, to know fully the Spirit of God in your brother.

4. It is only in the unity of the body that the Spirit of God can fully display His power, either in the church or to the world. God speaks to groups in ways He may never speak to individuals; there is generally a fuller tone, a more intense fervor, in public worship than in private worship, and as we know, there is greater joy in communion than can be realized in the most devout solitude.

Chapter 31

Be Filled
With the Spirit

And do not be drunk with wine, in which is dissipation;
but be filled with the Spirit, speaking to one another in
psalms and hymns and spiritual songs, singing and
making melody in your heart to the Lord.

Ephesians 5:18–19

These words are a command. They teach us not what the state of apostles or ministers ought to be, but what should be the consistent experience of every genuine believer. It is the privilege every child of God may claim from his Father—to be filled with the Spirit. Nothing less will enable him to live the life for which he has been redeemed: abiding in Christ, keeping His commandments, and bearing fruit. And yet how seldom has this command been counted among those to be kept at all costs! It has even been thought by some to be impossible or unreasonable that all should be expected to keep it.

No doubt one reason is that the words have been

misunderstood. Because on the day of Pentecost, and subsequent occasions, being filled with the Spirit was accompanied with supernatural manifestations, such a state has been looked upon as inconsistent with the normal Christian life. These manifestations, such as unknown tongues and flames of fire, have been so linked with the idea of being filled with the Spirit that it is often thought to be a blessing possible to only a few. Christians have felt they need not fix their hopes so high, as though if the blessing were given, it would be impossible to maintain it.

The message I would bring to you, my readers, is that the command is for every believer and that the promise and power are as sure as your redemption. May God give us grace in our meditation upon His Word not only to desire this blessing but also to have the assurance that the privilege is intended for all of us, that the way to it is not too difficult, and that the Spirit longs to indwell His people.

In countries such as South Africa, where I was born and where I have ministered for many years, we often suffer drought. There are two types of dams or reservoirs made for holding and storing water. On some farms there is a natural spring, but the stream is often too weak with which to irrigate the crops. A reservoir is constructed for collecting the water, and the filling of it is the result of the gentle, quiet inflow from the spring day and night. In other areas, farms have no natural springs, and so the reservoir is built in the bed of a stream or in a hollow where, when the rain falls, the water can be collected. In these places, the filling of the reservoir by a heavy rainfall is often accomplished in a few hours and is accompanied by a rushing, violent flow. The noiseless influx of water to the former farm is actually more certain, because, though quiet, the supply is steady and permanent. In tracts where the rainfall is scarce, a reservoir may stand empty for months or even years.

We can compare this to the way in which the fullness of the Spirit comes. As on the day of Pentecost, some outpourings of the Spirit are sudden, mighty, earth-shaking manifestations. These are like the rain-swollen reservoirs being filled suddenly. In contrast, the quiet presence of the Spirit when a soul is converted is steady and sure and yet not always so easily identified. The blessing is often greatly dependent on fellowship with others or extends only to the upper currents of the soul's life. But the sudden outpouring and infilling can be superficial, the depths of the will and inner life may not be touched. There are others who have never been present when such a marked manifestation of the Spirit occurs, but in whom the fullness of the Spirit is no less seen in deep devotion to Jesus, in a walk in the light of His countenance and consciousness of His presence, or in the blameless life of simple trust and obedience. They are like Barnabas: a son of consolation, a good man, and full of the Holy Spirit. Like the quiet springs, the Spirit flows and feeds the soul continually.

Which of these is the true way to be filled with the Spirit? The answer is simple. Just as there are farms in which each of the above-mentioned reservoirs are found, so there are individuals, some of whom have the steady infilling of the Spirit, while others have enjoyed mighty visitations of the Spirit. The regular, quiet, daily inflowing of a spring keeps a farm supplied in time of drought; in times of rain, the one equipped only with large reservoirs is ready to receive and store up large supplies. Blessed are those who can recognize God in both and keep themselves ready to be blessed in whatever way He chooses to come.

What are the conditions of the fullness of the Spirit? God's Word has one answer—faith. It is faith alone that sees and receives the invisible and that sees and receives God himself. The cleansing from sin and the loving surrender to obedience, which were the conditions of the first reception of the Spirit, are the fruit of the faith that sees what sin is, what the blood can do, and what the will and the love of God are. But we are not speaking here of this experience.

This word is for believers who have been faithful to obey but have not yet received what they long for. By faith they must discover what it is that needs to be cast out. Filling first requires an empty vessel. I am not speaking here of the cleansing of sin and the surrender to full obedience that is salvation. This is the first essential step. But I am speaking to believers who think they have done what God demands and yet fail to receive the blessing of the fullness of the Spirit. Remember, the first condition of filling is emptiness. What is a reservoir but a great hollow space—an emptiness—prepared, waiting, thirsting for the water to come. Any true abiding fullness of the Spirit is preceded by emptying. "I sought the blessing long and earnestly," said one, "and I wondered why it did not come. At last I found it was because there was no room in my heart to receive it." In such emptying there are various elements involved: a deep dissatisfaction with the "religion" we have had until now. A deep consciousness of how much there has been of the wisdom and work of the flesh. A discovery, confession, and giving up of all in own management, in which self has had control, of all in which we had not thought it necessary that Jesus be consulted or pleased. A deep conviction of our inability and utter helplessness to grasp or claim what has been offered. And finally a surrender in poverty of spirit to wait on the Lord for His great mercy and power. According to the riches of His glory, He will strengthen us by His Spirit in the inner man. We need a great longing, thirsting, waiting, praying without ceasing for the Father to fulfill His promise and to take full possession of us.

Together with this, we need the faith that accepts, receives, and maintains the gift. It is through faith in Christ and in the Father that the divine fullness will flow into us. Of the same Ephesians to whom the command was given "Be filled with the Spirit," Paul said, "In Christ, having believed, you were sealed with the Holy Spirit of promise." The command refers to what they had already received. The spring was within them, but it had to be opened up. It would then bubble up and fill their being. Yet this was effected in their own power. Jesus said, "He that believes in me, rivers of living water shall flow out of him." The fullness of the Spirit is so truly a revelation of Jesus; the receiving from Him must be in the unbroken continuity of a life fellowship. The ceaseless inflow of the sap from Him, the living vine, must be met by a consistently humble faith so that the releasing of the spring within is a result of our complete dependence on Jesus. By our faith in Jesus—whose baptism with the Spirit has as clear a beginning as His cleansing in the blood—we will know a continuous renewal in our own spirits.

Faith in Jesus and the constant sense of the Spirit does

not dispense with faith in the Father's gift and prayer for a renewed fulfillment of His promise. For the Ephesians, who had the Spirit within them as the pledge of their inheritance, Paul prays to the Father: "that He would grant you, according to the riches of His glory, to be strengthened with might through His Spirit in the inner man" (Ephesians 3:16). The verbs denote not a work, but an act—something done at once. The expression "according to the riches of His glory" indicates a great demonstration of divine love and power. They had the Spirit indwelling them. He prayed that the direct intervention of the Father would give them such a work of the Spirit, such a fullness of the Spirit, that the indwelling of Christ with His life of love that passes knowledge might be their personal experience.

At the time of the flood, the windows of heaven and the fountains of the great deep were opened together. The fulfillment of the promise of the Spirit is the same: "For I will pour water on him who is thirsty, and floods on the dry ground; I will pour My Spirit on your descendants, and My blessing on your offspring" (Isaiah 44:3). The deeper and clearer our faith in the indwelling Spirit, and the simpler the waiting on Him, the more abundant will be the renewed outpouring of the Spirit from the heart of the Father directly into the heart of His waiting child.

There is one more aspect in which it is essential to remember that this fullness comes by faith. God loves to appear in a humble, unlikely state, to be clothed in the garment of humility, which He also expects His children to love and wear. "The kingdom of heaven is like a seed": Only faith can know what glory there is in its smallness. Likewise was the dwelling of the Son on earth and so the indwelling of the Spirit in the heart. He asks that we believe in Him when we see and feel nothing. Believe that the fountain that springs up and flows forth in living streams is within you, even when all appears to be dry. Take time to retire into the inner chamber of your heart, and from there send up praise and offer worship to God in the assurance of the Holy Spirit within. Take time to be still and realize His presence; let the Spirit himself fill your spirit with this most wonderful truth: He dwells within you. Not first in the thoughts or feelings, but in the life—deeper than seeing and feeling, is His temple, His hidden dwelling place. When once faith knows that it has what it asks, it can afford to be patient and abound in thanksgiving even where the flesh would murmur. Faith trusts the unseen Jesus and the hidden Spirit. It can believe in that tiny, unlikely seed. It can trust and give glory to Him who is able to do exceedingly abundantly above all we can ask or think, and can strengthen the inner man just when all appears weak and ready to faint. Believer, don't expect the fullness of the Spirit to come in a way that your human reasoning devises, but as the coming of the Son of God without form or comeliness, in a way that is folly to human wisdom. Expect the divine strength in great weakness; humble yourself to receive the divine wisdom that the Spirit teaches; be willing to be nothing, because God chooses "the things that are not to bring to nothing the things that are." You will learn not to glory in the flesh but in the Lord. In the deep joy of a life of daily obedience and childlike simplicity, you shall know what it is to be filled with the Spirit.

O God, your fullness of love and glory is like a boundless ocean—infinite and inconceivable! I bless you that in revealing your Son, it pleased you that all the fullness of the Godhead should dwell in Him, that in Him we might see that fullness in human life and weakness. I bless you that His church on earth is even now, in all its weakness, His body, the fullness of Him that fills all in all; that in Him we are made full; that by the mighty working of your Spirit, and the indwelling of your Son, and the knowledge of your love, we may be filled with all the fullness of God.

I thank you, Father, that the Holy Spirit is to us the bearer of the fullness of Jesus and that in being filled with the Spirit we are made full with that fullness. I thank you that there have been many on earth since the day of Pentecost of whom you have said that they were full of the Holy Spirit. Make me full, too. Let the Holy Spirit take and keep possession of my deepest inmost life. Let your Spirit fill my spirit. Let the fountain flow from you through all my soul's affections and powers. Let it overflow my lips, speaking your praise and love. Let my body, by the quickening and sanctifying energy of the Spirit, be your temple, full of the divine life. Lord, I believe you have heard me. You have given it to me. I accept it as mine.

Now grant that throughout your church the fullness of the Spirit may be sought and found, known and proved. Lord Jesus, may your whole church be full of the Holy Spirit. Amen.

Summary

1. Being filled with the Spirit is not in the emotions. It is not in conscious light, power, or joy that the filling of the Spirit must first be sought, but in the hidden, inmost part of our being, deeper than knowledge or feeling—

the region to which faith alone has access and where we *are* and *have* before we know or feel.

2. Would you like to know what it is to be filled with the Spirit? Look at Jesus on His last night on earth: Knowing that the Father had given all things into His hands and that He was come from God and was going back to God, He washed the disciples' feet. We know that He was of God, full of the Holy Spirit. And He sent the Spirit to us so that we too might be full of Him.

3. Notice carefully the connection: "Be filled with the Spirit, *speaking to one another.*" It is in the fellowship of the body and its being built up in love that the Spirit reveals His presence. Jesus said, "The Spirit shall bear witness, and you shall bear witness." It is in activity on our part—in obedience—that the full consciousness of the Spirit's presence comes. "They were filled with the Holy Spirit, and began to speak." Having the same Spirit of faith, therefore, we speak. The fountain must spring up; the stream must flow. Silence is death.

4. Do not grieve the Holy Spirit of God. This word precedes "Be filled with the Spirit." We cannot cause the life or the growth, but we can remove the hindrances. We can act in obedience; we can turn from the flesh to wait upon God; we can yield to the Spirit as far as we know God's will. *The filling comes from above.* Wait for it, tarry at the foot of the throne in prayer. And as you pray, believe that His unseen power has full possession of your being.

5. "Be filled with the Spirit." It is the duty, the calling, the

privilege of every believer—a divine possibility in virtue of the command, a divine certainty in the power of faith. God hasten the day when every believer will know and believe this word.

 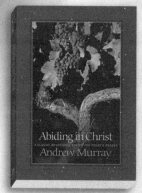 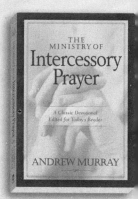
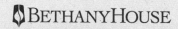